2

RIV

D0131187

Gardening
With
Wildlife

Copyright © 1974 National Wildlife Federation. All rights reserved. Reproduction of the whole or any part of the contents without written permission is prohibited.

Library of Congress CIP Data: page 189

Least Chipmunk (*Eutamias minimus*) by Donald Titus

Gardening With Wildlife

A Complete Guide to
Attracting and Enjoying
The Fascinating Creatures
In Your Backyard

NATIONAL WILDLIFE FEDERATION

Contents

Tiger Swallowtail *(Papilio glaucus)* on Rhododendron by Grant Heilman

Introduction

Man's deep-rooted kinship with the earth is nowhere more clearly seen than in the satisfaction he has always found in making a garden. The meanings of this creative act were recorded in mythology, literature, and art long before modern science began to measure the gardener's labors and tell him how to get better results.

But whether it was to grow vegetables for the table, to construct an elaborate bower for royal pageantry, or to create today's inviting outdoor living-room, man's goal has usually been to please himself in his garden. Striving for total control, he includes that which enhances his life-style, and excludes all else—often even the wildlife on which the perpetuation of plant life may ultimately depend. It is this drive to manipulate his environment, extended from garden to field to plains to mountains, that has brought man to a global crisis of environmental misuse.

That is why the National Wildlife Federation, in its search for ways by which everyone can help restore a harmonious relationship between man and the earth, addresses a book to gardeners. Hoping to extend the gardener's respect and feeling for the soil to the whole magnificent ecosystem of which it is a part, we have asked biologists, craftsmen, artists, and educators to tell why and how they share their green space—even their vegetable gardens—with wildlife. Although their words and pictures focus on the birds, small mammals, and amphibians of the urban East, their ideas apply to gardens throughout the land. As dedicated conservationists, they know the urgency of keeping enough of our environment habitable for wildlife to insure that man may continue to live here as well.

Whether in backyard, mountain canyon, or forest vale, wildlife is an integral part of the grand scheme of things. Where it finds its requirements for life, it survives—to delight the artist, thrill the photographer, challenge the hunter, and fill our mundane lives with color, music, and excitement.

Our children's children may yet enjoy that legacy if we will open the garden gate and welcome wildlife back into our everyday lives where it belongs.

Thomas L. Kimball
Executive Vice-President
National Wildlife Federation

A birdhouse she built herself, a child's way of saying, "Welcome to our garden!" is acknowledged with thanks in nature's silent code. Each rustle and chirp within bespeaks the mystery and dignity of all life and an orderliness of which she is herself a part.

Photo by Jerry Imber

From Gardens
Old and New—
An Invitation

Re-stocking the bird feeder
Adding a flower-splashed corner to the backyard habitat; photos by David W. Corson

Antique birdhouse circa 1816

Generations ago a Virginian raised this gracious birdhouse on a post—and birds have adorned his yard ever since. Shady neighborhoods attract wildlife best; birds nest or rest in the big trees and soon spot the birdbath glinting below in a riot of iris. But in old homes or new, in city or suburb, wherever a family fills a feeder and tends a garden, it puts out the welcome mat for wildlife.

Birdbath in iris bed by Paul Genereux

Red Squirrel *(Tamiasciurus hudsonicus)* by Pat Wheat/Bruce Coleman, Inc.

Green Snake *(Opheodrys sp.)* by Heather R. Iler

Young Katydid *(Scudderia sp.)* by Heather R. Iler

The Response from Curious Wildlife– Thank you!

They come not to please you, but because you have pleased them— sometimes in ways you hadn't meant. Shoo, red squirrel; those seeds are for birds! But the birds will wing in soon enough. The snake will explore the chrysanthemums, the katydid measure a geranium, the chipmunk and a brace of frogs inspect you from their doorsteps. Having them near is thanks enough for your care.

Green Frog *(Rana clamitans)* by Grant Heilman

Eastern Chipmunk *(Tamias striatus)*
by Leonard Lee Rue III/Bruce Coleman, Inc.

11

Even When Winter Comes, the Welcome Mat's Out

Cardinals *(Richmondena cardinalis)* by Heather R. Iler

Filling a pine cone feeder with peanut butter
by Kent and Donna Dannen

Ring-necked Pheasant *(Phasianus colchicus)* and Eastern Gray Squirrel *(Sciurus carolinensis)* by Grant Heilman

Replenishing backyard wildlife feeders by Kent and Donna Dannen

Providing food for brushpile residents by Larry West

Our commitment to wildlife spans four seasons and 50 states. Nature lovers in Colorado, Maryland, and Michigan bundle up against winter's cold to feed their wild neighbors against winter's dearth. Suet, seed, and peanut butter dabbed into a pine cone will bring a flutter of wings to the edge of a porch. Cardinals paint the snow red at a freshly stocked feeder which baffled squirrels can't raid. Birds and a ring-necked pheasant hen must wait as the gray squirrel has his hour at grain strewn on the snow. Apples and lettuce make a gourmet's banquet for hungry tenants in a drifted brushpile. And beyond suburbia an off-duty birdbath and an outsized feeder box get a refill for bigger visitors, the deer.

Hold Your Breath and Watch: Visitors from the Woods

From the warmth behind a picture window we watch the deer accept our gifts. Perhaps we have only varied their diet of winter browse— or perhaps we have actually softened the rigors of a severe winter. Either way, we acknowledge the debt we owe to creatures large and small whose habitats we have sawn and bulldozed to make room for ourselves. But nature holds no grudges; we have only to invite them back and they will come to country garden, suburban yard, or city window box—soaring, crawling, paddling, walking into realms we all can share.

Mule Deer (*Odocoileus hemionus*)
by Kent and Donna Dannen

by Leonard Lee Rue III

by Leonard Lee Rue III

by David W. Corson

by Grant Heilman

Roger Tory Peterson by Russ Kinne

1 | Your Guide to Garden Wildlife

By Roger Tory Peterson

A solitary robin hopped to another spot on the lawn, cocked its head, and deftly plucked a worm. Overhead a blue jay scolded, contesting a squirrel's right to the leftover acorns at the foot of the tree. A honey bee reveled in the rich pollen of a daffodil, packing bits of gold into back-leg baskets.

The wildlife in my garden literally hummed with activity as I pondered the National Wildlife Federation's invitation to write the introductory chapter to their book on backyard and garden wildlife. What an appealing idea—even for me, not noted for my horticulture. Still, I once wrote "the imaginative gardener sows his borders not only with red, pink, and yellow hollyhocks, but also with red cardinals, rosy purple finches, and yellow grosbeaks."

Yet—the idea of gardening with wildlife—what a seeming contradiction! How can wildlife be called wild if content to live within the fences of our residential plots and by the terms of our automobile-centered landscapes? Surely we are talking about domesticated creatures with no more wildness than a lapdog's. Such reservations are foolish: the sky is wide open to all who would fly into my air space; the soil is a subterranean throughway rather than a barrier for those who would enter my garden by the low road; nor have I ever built a picket fence that can stop the rabbit family to whom this piece of turf has always belonged. Oh yes, it is mine, but it remains theirs for they are of the earth.

Admittedly, the eagle seldom soars above my gables and no mountain lion peers forth from my dahlias. Rainbow trout have not once broken the placid surface of my pool. But wildlife fierce and noble as lords of the Serengeti lurks in every niche of my yard.

You doubt it? If slaughter-rate is your measurement of wildness, I give you the ladybug larva which eats its weight in aphids any summer day. If a

Roger Tory Peterson, pictured (opposite) on the garden steps of his Old Lyme, Connecticut, home is world famous as a wildlife author and artist, and as the originator of the "Peterson" system of field recognition of birds. Although he travels to many exotic parts of the world, he still finds inspiration for his art from watching the array of wildlife visitors which grace his backyard throughout the year.

ferocious mask convinces you of a wild heart within, I give you the praying mantis, or perhaps the frog-targeted garden snake. Nor do snakes' and insects' savagery surpass that of the barred owl or great horned owl when a rustled leaf betrays a mouse (both owls visit my property at night so I know their killing habits well). The expectable behavior patterns of the robin, chipmunk, and honeybee may seem tame, but they actually involve an inexorable struggle for survival and growth—a struggle that is very much our business.

Like me, you are in possession momentarily of a garden, or at least a crabgrass ecosystem. Philosophically you may deny it, intending to move on and get away again, feeling no involvement with nature at this point in time. Perhaps you are swept by our industrial society's contagion—a disbelief in the importance of your own contribution, a trust only in things that click on and off at the touch of your fingers. My urgent plea is that you snap out of it, that you claim your kinship with the creatures awaiting outside your back door, for your own sake as well as theirs.

Toward a Natural America

The National Wildlife Federation has long served as an information transmitter between scientists studying wildlife in the field and the public. It is therefore admirable that, in a newly opened sector of its activities, the Federation is inviting the public to join the scientists not only in observing, but in supplying the needs of wildlife. Biologists are now observing with fascination America's backyard effort to restore wildlife habitats. Sparked by a recent story in *National Wildlife* magazine, the Federation's Backyard Wildlife Program (see page 184—Ed.) provides encouragement and advice to all who seek to be a part of the environmental revolution.

Not long ago flower gardens, with their formal beds and elaborate variety, offered proper settings chiefly for professional gardener-botanists and leisurely dilettantes. For the latter, it was a lovely world of prizewinning gladioli, fragrant grape arbors, and espaliered pear trees. Even the working areas had their charm: greenhouses and potting sheds with sinks and shelves and racks for hanging the particular implement at its honored place.

Now Jefferson's common man has become the gardener. Indeed, the popular surge of interest in the natural way of living has become the outstanding phenomenon of the seventies. And not merely for young people with a copy of *Foxfire* in their backpacks. Sales of vegetable seeds are up; the hardware store thrives in the down-turned economy. Not since the Victory Gardens of World War II have American families so dedicated themselves to turning the soil as a group effort. The people's culture celebrates not only Dr. deBakey who heals the human heart, but Dr. Craighead who has taken the grizzly's pulse (on the theory that if the bear survives, so can we).

The great horned owl is the largest of the eared owls. But the "ears" are feather tufts which serve no functional purpose. This big bird is usually found in deep forests, but may also live in city parks where it helps to control rats and mice.

What the backyard program offers is not a misty-eyed image of an ethereal land—an Arcadian dream—for people of pure hearts. Rather it proposes an organic culture in which everyone can play a part. But before describing the specific activities which gardening with wildlife opens up to American families, I'd like to say a bit more about the scientific process that's involved. It's not just a matter of giving back to the soil many of the nutrients which we over the years have taken from it—and thereby gaining ever more enriched vegetables, more beautiful flowers, and greater numbers of backyard wildlife. It's also a matter of contemporary Americans realizing that they are making a contribution toward the evolution of our continent's flora and fauna—a contribution that can be positive rather than negative.

What stood on your land when the first settlers arrived? In those days, legend says, a squirrel could leap from limb to limb all the way from the Atlantic coast across the Appalachians to the Mississippi shore. Since then so much has changed: the magnificent flowering chestnut has virtually disappeared, wiped out by a fungus accidentally introduced to New York State from Europe in 1904; the elms of New England may soon become a tribal memory (it happens that their fatal disease was also an import, from Holland); black walnut trees with that hard and beautifully grained wood have fallen victim to the passion of cabinetmakers.

Yet this evolutionary sequence, the story of the greenery that has been phased out of existence in our country in the last two centuries, is but a fleeting moment in the whole drama. Even the most primitive trees, grasses, and flowers began to develop on earth only 420 million years ago, as against the earth's entire 4.5 billion years of development. The flowering trees, the trees which we see about us today, emerged perhaps 100 million years later and marked a major evolutionary triumph for all life forms. Previously trees had

The magnificent grizzly bear of the Rocky Mountains has been the object of research by scientists. The gathering of physiological and behavioral data, information on movement patterns, and analysis of habitat requirements may determine its chance for survival in the future.

been but oversized ferns, haphazard in reproduction (by spores), greenery which would have been quite inhospitable to the kinds of wildlife seen in your backyard and mine. Similarly, grasses and flowers have evolved over the millenia by a series of happy accidents or favorable Providence, giving us sun-dappled gardens, more-or-less dependable lawns, and the makings of good wildlife habitat.

Evolution of another sort has occurred in the relationship between beast and man, animals whose kinship was so idealistically portrayed in that marvelous primitive painting, "The Peaceable Kingdom." Some 35,000 years ago, our Stone Age ancestors were proclaiming their worshipful allegiance to certain life-giving animals by depicting them on the walls of caves in France and Spain. Later, somewhere in the Middle East, early farmers (who had already turned the corner into civilization by means of plow-pulling bullocks) succeeded in breeding a domesticated version of the Asian jungle fowl (*Gallus gallus*), mother of all modern hens. On this continent, the American Indians demonstrated their gratitude to the wolf, the bear, and the beaver by giving those names to their tribal clans and those faces to their totems. Unavoidably, perhaps, glaciers and the Indians' Ice Age ancestors brought the woolly mammoths and the sabre-toothed tigers to extinction. Proliferating Americans of the 19th century virtually eliminated the buffalo and drove into extinction the passenger pigeon and the Carolina parakeet.

Yet the effect of man on animal life in North America has not always been adverse. The cardinal and the mockingbird have actually extended their ranges along with our urban growth, adapting beautifully to the man-dominated world. In fact, they and many other birds even prefer our shrubs and hedges to the depths of undisturbed forests. And though the current conservation movement can never bring back the great auk or Audubon's bighorn, it may succeed in saving the Florida manatee, the red wolf, and the whooping crane.

Now we stand at a crossroad of time: our awareness of what we have been doing unconsciously to our natural environment meets with a widespread recognition that we are indeed powerful agents. We have the potential to reestablish a life-giving relationship with animals just as we have the potential to fill our landscapes with beauty. And this realization occurs, fittingly, at the 200th anniversary of our nation's birth, at a moment when we should be of a mind to rediscover or recreate the richness of the American land as well as of the American spirit.

A Role for the Gardener

Perhaps the preservation of a roosting place for your neighborhood owl is not so exciting as fastening a tracking device on a grizzly. But many of the decisions you must make for the good of the owl are equally complex.

The screech owl's silent swooping attack is launched after split-second scrutiny of the intended victim. Equipped with pupils which dilate abruptly, its eyes enable the owl to see small rodents and insects first in maximum light, and the next instant in razor-sharp focus, before it plunges earthward for the kill. As the owl strikes, its bending legs reflexively close the talons around the struggling prey. An inhabitant of open woodlands, the screech owl's name belies its most often used call, a soft, whirring whinny.

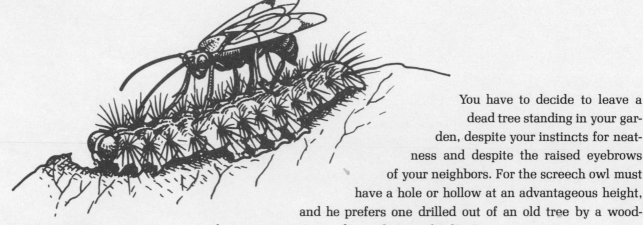

The female of the wasp species,
Apanteles melanoscelus, in the short
month of her adult life, will lay a
single egg in each of hundreds
of gypsy moth larvae. Such
parasitized caterpillars eat at less
than half their normal destructive
rate and die about a week after
the growing wasp maggot chews its
way out of its host.

You have to decide to leave a dead tree standing in your garden, despite your instincts for neatness and despite the raised eyebrows of your neighbors. For the screech owl must have a hole or hollow at an advantageous height, and he prefers one drilled out of an old tree by a woodpecker. Are you going to leave the tree for him?

To make such a decision demands information—and that is the purpose of this book. Its authors intend to give the guidelines and the techniques necessary for you to create a backyard habitat which will help to preserve and support a greater diversity of native wildlife in your region. Throughout the book you will be encouraged to form a natural relationship with, rather than to dominate, the land you own. For if you replenish lost nutrients and replant certain native, hardy plants, the land will, of itself, develop a life-sustaining ecosystem for a variety of wildlife. The authors' basic assumption is that wildlife and you will make good neighbors.

A few years ago we had the great locust scare in the East. Let us salute, in retrospect, the knowledgeable gardeners and conservationists of Wilton, Connecticut, who refused to let the town spray their trees with insecticide against the cicadas. They feared the consequences of spraying among birds and other wildlife. In a few short weeks the cicadas went away, as the well-read citizens knew they would, not to appear for another 17 years, leaving the trees not much weakened by the depredation.

The plague of the gypsy moth is still with us. Again exponents of both chemical and biological control methods square off, ready to claim infested acres as their own laboratories. Increasingly, the trend is toward integration of both, with caution and moderation the watchwords. Realizing that the gypsy moth came to this continent from Europe, biologists have sought out one of its traditional predators there, the wasp *Apanteles melanoscelus,* and are expanding earlier experiments with it, along with refined forms of viruses which act specifically on the gypsy moth. Biologists are hopeful of success, and the wasp seems to be another successful American immigrant.

Stop, Look, Listen—to Nature

For many years, I have been saying that the long-run ecological solutions of such pest problems will increasingly bring nature back into the act as the farmer's partner. This assumes, of course, that the gardener-farmer knows what he's doing, and that he's as willing as a wildlife ranger at a national park to make an objective, rather than sentimental, decision in the interests of good management. We are indeed asking you to regard your own quarter acre—or whatever your yard's dimensions—together with its flora and fauna, as a part of the American commonwealth. For the time you own it, you are the custodian of a piece of earth which is, by prior right and natural law, a small or large part of the home range of a myriad of other living organisms.

As man, you have the power and the knowledge to extinguish the life support system of these other species. Or you can choose to improve your section of their habitat and offer them continued life. In order to have more than a minimal impact you will also have to encourage your neighbors and your community to plant and manage their land with the needs of wildlife in mind. We ask you to become a serious and knowledgeable amateur in studying your land and the larger environment of which it is a part, improving it where possible, and appreciating it for its changes, as well as its timeless consistencies.

In this process, the first and most important step is to start making a log book. What animals have you seen where and doing what in your garden? Which vegetation was involved? At what time of day? What was the weather like? Were the seasons changing? How did the other animals react? Does this represent something new, or is it consistent with the part of the country where you live?

How to Tell a Moth from a Butterfly

Let me try to help you with your naturalist's log by giving a few hints as to how you may learn to identify who is who in your garden. This has been my own particular role, to make it relatively easy for the layman to become a competent and well-informed bird spotter. I have done this by reducing the plethora of identification criteria offered by systematic ornithologists down to a few simple visual points. The same technique works in kingdoms other than the birds'. In advising anyone how to tell a moth from a butterfly, for instance, I would ask him to discover whether the creature in question was plump-bodied, furry, and had pointed, feathered antennae. Also, was it observed at night? If it conforms to this, it's probably a moth. The often brilliantly colored butterfly by contrast, is seen by day, has a slender body, and waves slender, knobbed antennae.

But perhaps before focusing on details we should first review some fundamental principles—which merely involves putting name tags on the nine or ten major animal groups you'll find represented in your garden. Only nine or ten? Yes, and you already know them. There are the birds, mammals, reptiles, amphibians, and insects, as well as classes represented by spiders, "bugs" with many legs (centipedes and millipedes), earthworms, mollusks, and crustaceans.

You may also know a good deal about the biological characteristics of these several groups; what makes a worm a worm, for example. You know that it

A nature log, faithfully kept, becomes an increasingly valuable record. Besides enabling you to plan better for next year—and settling arguments about what happened last year—the act of writing it down forces you to become a more astute observer.

has a segmented body (having in your youth probably tried the experiment of cutting one of the wrigglers in half and seeing that both parts usually survived). But do you know how a worm gets its oxygen? Through its skin, from air spaces in the soil. And were you aware that this humble creature also possesses five pairs of hearts?

You may also remember from a childhood picking-up-bugs phase that the fundamental difference between a centipede and millipede is that the former has one pair of legs per segment while the latter has two. Also, that the less leggy fellow has poison glands and long antennae while the leggier one isn't poisonous and has short antennae.

You may, on the other hand, claim a lack of familiarity with mollusks and crustaceans, doubting that you are sharing your garden with them. If you've got snails or slugs, you've got mollusks. If you've noticed some clam-like looking creatures in your freshwater pond, you've got another kind of mollusk, probably a pond mussel. Crustaceans range from tiny ephemera like the fairy shrimp (shown on page 108) to such mini-monsters as crayfish. Dry-land crustaceans, on the other hand, include those sowbugs and potato bugs which you discover under rocks and logs. Their familiar characteristics include being segmented and wearing their skeletons on their *outsides*. The border lines between the ten animal groups are quite clearly drawn, as clearly as the difference between bird and mammal. We mammals, of course, all have four limbs and a certain amount of hair; we tend to drink first from our mother's breast. Among our mammalian relatives, the rodents are represented in the garden in particular strength by chipmunk, squirrel, and mouse. Then there are insect-eating mammals like the mole and the shrew, and the gnawing mammals which, in your garden, include the rabbit and the hare. Birds differ from mammals in their feathered skins and their reproductive technique.

Among the reptiles, eggs are also the most common reproductive technique. The offspring of these cold-blooded animals are always miniature replicas of the adults. That is not true of the amphibians, which, while equally cold-blooded, are hatched in water in different, larval form, emerging finally to a terrestrial life only after a gradual metamorphosis. What child has not been entranced by the budding of hind legs on a captive tadpole!

For the insects, there is an even greater developmental difference: many of them pass through two or three stages of metamorphosis before attaining adult form. Another characteristic of an insect is that its body is divided into three sections—the head, the thorax, and the abdomen. Spiders have two-part bodies (the head and thorax forming one section and the abdomen the

Children take a special delight in watching nature's busy world, and wise parents will encourage and enrich this innate curiosity. Providing necessary equipment and making informative books available are two means by which the spark of interest may be fanned.

other), four pairs of legs, and no antennae. They also possess poison glands with which they can paralyze their prey.

A Checklist Helps

I have always preferred to concentrate on certain easy-to-spot field marks rather than on the technical, taxonomic differences among wildlife's phyla and classes and orders. When dealing with an identification problem (such as: I know that's a mammal, but is it a woodchuck or a gopher?), I set aside scientific perspectives and run down this list of eight questions:

      1. What's its size?

      2. What's its shape in silhouette?

      3. What's its dominant color?

      4. Are there special field marks?

      5. How does it behave?

      6. How does it move?

      7. What sound does it make?

      8. Where does it live?

Then, with the answers, I turn to a field guide and can tell for sure that . . . it's a gopher!

With tiny insects, some of these questions may seem a bit gross. Admittedly, it's hard to say much about a gnat's distinctive markings or appendages. But I would nonetheless recommend that you try; it's relatively easy if you acquire a ten-times magnifying glass. With it, you can enter into the green world, spotting such crucial differences as whether an insect has wings, how many, and their shape—finding clues comparable to variations in beaks or feet or flight patterns in the bird world. Soon you'll be 'way beyond assessing the general body shape of the insect and will be discerning the complexity of the eyes, the number of veins in the wings, and whether the antennae have knobs.

The observation of insect behavior is no dull pastime. Far from it. Ever since early boyhood I have been fascinated by the economy and society of ants; their relationships with each other and with their enemies, their storage of food in different seasons, and their preparation of seemingly vast military campaigns. Mammals are just as fascinating when you observe them carefully. How far from its den will a squirrel roam in search of food? What kind of chatter does it make under different conditions? And why do you never see one at night by flashlight—or have you? This is, for me, the golden dividend earned from observing backyard wildlife: gaining an understanding of the relationship between an animal's peculiarities and his corner of my garden.

Yet eventually for me the study of birds' behavior became particularly rewarding. From few aspects of human endeavor do I gain as much satis-

Nature will bear the closest inspection: she invites us to lay our eye level with the smallest leaf and take an insect view of its plain. Every part is full of life.

    —Henry David Thoreau

faction as from watching, for example, the carryings on of a flock of cedar waxwings—those beautifully crested, sleek berry-snatchers which arrive on a ripe tree like legionnaires at a convention. Pushing shoulder to shoulder in their eager pursuit of the fruit, they'll hang upside down to get into a favored position against their competitors. But (have you noticed this?) at other times, they may seem to change their ways and be considerate of one another, passing a cherry from bill to bill.

Looking at my garden as a whole, I view a tree as a distinct neighborhood—a "quality subdivision." Each maple, oak, or pine hosts a variety of tenants, from microscopic larvae to large-scaled predators. Chipmunks burrow between the roots, raccoons and squirrels den in the hollows, beetles drill the bark, then birds devour both beetle and bud—a cooperative living arrangement which never ceases to amaze and delight me.

Yet the enjoyment of your backyard's related habitats involves more than just sitting still with your eyes open and your notebook at hand. Having even a beginner's knowledge of what's supposed to be happening in each portion of the habitat helps. "Supposed to happen" is, of course, a moralistic phrase that would shock a real scientist. I'm talking, more accurately, about the balance of nature. And in that balance, the most active character, more likely the hero than the villain, is the insect.

The Unlikely Hero

He looks, as various writers have remarked, as if he had come from another planet—with neither the engaging grace nor heartwarming habits of our furry and feathered friends. But actually he is more of this earth than we are, in the sense that he has been here longer (and may survive longer) than we mammals. Specifically, the first insect anteceded our most ancient forebear by some 350 million years; some of them in all the subsequent millenia have altered not a whit, while many others have adapted their forms in the most ingenious and persistent ways to new conditions imposed on this old earth. Because of their adaptability insects have never really lost their commanding role; they are the dominant life form anywhere on this globe. In the United States, for instance, the number of species of insects is probably a hundred times greater than the number of bird species. Perhaps it is for this quality, the inextinguish-ability of insects, as well as for their vast numbers, that we poor mortals view them as so threatening. "Quick, Henry, the *Flit!*" an advertisement used to warn. But often, like Lady Macbeth's spot, the insect won't be rubbed out—and it's a good thing it won't. Indiscriminate eradication of insects makes no sense either

The cedar waxwing's passion for fruit such as cherries and red cedar berries, can make him seem greedy at times. Although they commonly nest in the Northeast and winter in the South, a flock of waxwings seem to turn up almost any place where berries are ripe.

*Carnivorous insects and spiders
combine stealth with a formidable
array of poison beaks, sucking tubes,
and spiked pincers to capture, kill,
and devour other insects and spiders.*

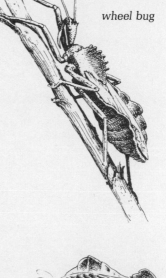

wheel bug

ecologically or economically. They provide indispensable services by pollinating plants and breaking down waste materials, services which more than balance their account to the good in the garden.

I've read of some little beetles which successfully toughed it out for 12 years in a bottle of a very strong poison. This hard-shelled penchant for survival is truly more to be admired than feared. Keep two things in mind as you ponder the stubborn beetle: first, he and countless species of insects native to North America are essential in several ways to the life systems of many of the plants and animals on which we depend; second, he and his kind only get out of control and expand alarmingly when there is a radical change in the fixed, natural, predator-prey relationships of a given habitat. Where no birds sing, the insects ravage.

ambush bug

Is it for their predators' benefit or for their own survival that insects are so prolific? Take your choice. But prolific they certainly are: a honeybee queen is quite capable of laying 2,000 eggs in a day; an aphid family (those pale green insects on your rosebush) can bring forth ten generations in a year. And how beneficial aphids are to that well-known tenant of your garden, the black ant! They provide the ants with honeydew, of which a sturdy aphid "cow" can produce four dozen delicious drops a day. The ants literally milk an aphid—by stroking its back with their antennae —to encourage the flow. If you're persistent and lucky, you can observe this exchange taking place. You can also ascertain that ants think well enough of their aphid cows to herd them into crude sheds built of leaves and grass.

robber fly

Beyond aphids, along with cicadas and other plant-juice sucking bugs, there are only about seven other insect orders represented in your garden. So don't despair of being able to keep track of what manner of tiny hero you're dealing with. Two other groups of plant-eaters (but don't worry about plant-eaters; we do it, too!) are the jumping insects and the social insects. Examples of the jumpers are those marvelous performers, the grasshopper and cricket; the social insects include the ant, bee, and wasp. And if you've forgotten everything you knew as a child about the difference between a wasp and a bee, I'll remind you that the former has a long, slender body with no hair, and a straight stinger, whereas the latter has a thick, hairy body, and a barbed stinger on its back. You probably remember that, though the stings differ in severity, the rule is: don't fool with either one!

flower spider and syrphid fly

Camouflage as a Way of Life

Within the various insect orders we find many adaptations to distinctive habitats. These include not only different dietary habits, but also variations in color and form. Of these, camouflage is a survival technique that holds a special fascination for me, an artist who makes his living by persuading

doodlebug

27

breeding plumage of male bobolink

the beholder that he sees something that isn't really there. For the walkingstick, the treehopper, and the katydid, the problem is just the reverse; they must persuade the beholder that he doesn't see something that *is* there. Yet artists they are, undoubtedly. I've even seen a walkingstick carry its act of mimicry to the point that it fell to the ground precisely like a dead twig. What bird would want to eat a twig?

An insect which I find particularly impressive is the eyed elater beetle (pictured on page 58). It is easily recognized by the two big spots on its thorax and by the salt-and-pepper color of the rest of its body. Unlike most of the large beetle fraternity, this particular click beetle, when upside down, is able to turn itself back right side up. By an adaptation of its segmented thorax, it seems to arch its back, then flip over onto its feet. Whenever it flips, it clicks; hence its name.

Three other important insect orders in your garden are the moths and butterflies, the flies which have two wings (unlike the four-winged, *true* bugs), and the dragonflies and damselflies which are often found hovering about your pond. It's particularly interesting to watch how the dragonfly and other carnivorous or omnivorous insects munch their food. The dragonfly nymph or naiad—which spends its existence in the water—has a grotesque "lower lip" which converts instantly from its folded position into an extended grappling hook. All at once the big lip zips out, zaps a victim, and pulls it in to the hard, sharp jaws for the kill. The voracious praying mantis seizes its meal in spiked forelegs, then takes a fatal bite. After chewing the delicacy with teeth-like grinders, it neatly cleans its spikes and washes its face. The ambush bug (pictured on page 27) also seizes and holds its prey with spiked forelegs. But this grotesque little creature has an even more bizarre way of dispatching its victim. A pointed tube unfolds from under the head, penetrates and drains the captive's body of its fluid as efficiently as if sipping through a straw.

But How Do You Find Them?

Let me try to summarize specifically where and when, and doing what, you may find all these awesome insects—secrets which the birds in your garden already know by heart. In and around the water you will find the mayfly, dragonfly, springtail, and water strider. Hiding in greenery you may find the camouflaged treehopper and walkingstick. Engaged in predatory pursuits you can find the praying mantis, the ant lion, and the robberfly. Dusk brings out the moths and fireflies. If you listen carefully, you will become aware of the crickets, katydids, cicadas, bumblebees, and mosquitoes. With patience you may see lacewing larvae, immediately upon com-

Although the bobolink is an open field bird, its nest of dried leaves, weed stems, and grasses is hard to find. Tucked into a slight depression in the ground, it is well-hidden by tall plants. The female further safeguards the young by running at least ten feet from the nest before flushing.

male's spring plumage

male's winter plumage resembles female's

28

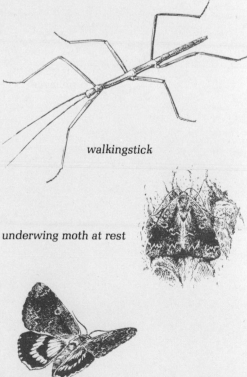

true katydid

thorn-like tree hopper

pine sphinx larva

caterpillar

ing to life, join the ladybugs in feeding on the nearby aphids which are also herded by the ants. What a remarkable world one sees through the magnifying glass!

A Checklist of Bird Habitats

Happily, birds are much easier to spot. You have probably already detected the five different areas of the garden environment in which different species are normally seen—because certain birds are adapted to survive best in those sections. We could label such denizens of special areas as follows:

Users of Buildings—These are generally the ledge and hole nesters of the bird kingdom—the robin, phoebe, starling, sparrow, house and Carolina wren, the chimney swift, and less frequently, the barn owl.

Bush and Hedge Dwellers—These include the cardinal, mockingbird, catbird, chipping sparrow, song sparrow, and yellow warbler.

Lawn Foragers—Among these you can recognize the starlings, grackles, robins, various sparrows, mourning doves, the occasional red-winged blackbird, and always juncos in winter.

Inhabitants of Wooded Areas—Here are various flycatchers, nuthatches, woodpeckers, warblers, grosbeaks, finches, and the tufted titmouse.

Pond and Stream Lovers—The variety of birds found feeding and nesting around water depends greatly on the size of the pond and its surrounding environment. Swallows will frequent the air spaces above water in search of insects. If the pond is bounded by sedges and grasses, it may provide nest sites for a few ducks, a marsh wren, or even a small heron.

Camouflage is insect survival insurance. The katydid, pine sphinx moth larva, and other caterpillars use leaf-like hues and markings. Treehoppers, clinging head down, look like thorns, and walkingsticks pass for twigs. The underwing moth conceals its bright hind wings with dull fore wings when it alights.

How do I explain that the mourning dove forages on the lawn and tends not to go mosquito-hunting over the pond? How do I rationalize that the bittern seeks the water and ignores the field? We must again repair to evolution for an answer (or to what we now grasp of evolution). The bittern surely looks the way it does, with striations to match the reeds among which it conceals itself, because it has lived in swampy regions for so many millenia. Natural selection has decreed it. The bobolink is surely such a consistent and successful resident of the meadow nearby (to which it returns after a migration all the way from South America) because it has, over countless generations, developed coloration and behavior which protect it from the hovering hawk and the lurking fox.

We have come to know much, but we still have much to learn. I do not know, for instance, why some birds have developed such magnificent vocal organs while others are so very poorly endowed. Nor why a great number of birds engage in "anting"—a ritual process of annointing their feathers with whole or crushed ants. Maybe you'll be able to decipher that puzzling behavior for me.

Observations by professional and amateur alike have begun to supply

walkingstick

underwing moth at rest

underwing moth in flight

Territoriality in birds of the same species is thought to serve the purpose of population control and assurance of an adequate food supply in a given area. Aside from singing to attract a mate and protect its turf, a bird also has several call notes which warn of impending danger, ask for assistance, or announce the discovery of a plentiful food source for other birds.

ethologists with much-needed information on how birds relate to each other. Do they make good neighbors—for each other? One bird spotter, Margaret Morse Nice, by keeping her eye on the song sparrows outside her window in Ohio, became one of the world's recognized authorities on their behavior. Other observers, working alone or in groups, have logged sufficient bird counts and activity descriptions to enable ornithologists to figure out specific patterns of territoriality. In my own immediate area, I've perceived that eight pairs of robins and three pairs of orioles, after a good deal of having-at each other and loud declamatory singing, have worked out a neighborhood *modus vivendi*.

How do they do it? The song of a bird is primarily a social expression. As the male sings, the female responds, signifying willingness to be a partner. But another male, perceiving in the song a threat, flies back to his own territory. From that secure perch, he hurls back his own challenging song. This utterly serious exchange of warnings and counter-challenges—which many listeners naively assume to be the birds' expression of the joy of living —will often continue across the males' shared boundary for hours. Meanwhile some females also join in the maintenance of the family territory by driving off other females.

It's a mistake, of course, to look for the same behavior from every type of bird. Although they all evolved from a reptilian ancestor many millions of years ago, selection and adaptation have produced an astonishing variety of feathered creatures. "What a diversity of finches!" exclaimed Darwin when he visited the Galapagos Islands. While there are many more than 20 orders of birds, most of those we see and hear in the garden belong to the order of perching birds. Woodpeckers may visit the garden but are not in the perching bird category. Neither is the mourning dove. Watch the crowd drinking at your birdbath and you'll see that every bird raises its head in order to swallow—with one exception, the dove. It's different. So, in other ways, are the swifts and hummingbirds. Birds of the other groups are more often observed swooping along the shore or soaring over the mountain ridges than in the garden.

Bird Look-Alikes

Don't let the wonderful variety of birds discourage you from getting acquainted with the comparatively small number of species which you will find nesting and feeding in your yard. Just remember my eight simple questions and repair to your field guides. However, I may be able to save you some seemingly impossible mix-ups in identifying similar birds if you will keep these identity clues in mind:

• The *starling* is the only black bird in your garden with a yellowish beak and a short tail. Don't confuse him with the *grackle*, which is a bit larger, has a dark beak, and a slightly longer tail, or with the *cowbird*, which has a brown head upon his black body.

• The *house sparrow* has a short, canary-like beak, and may often be observed "dust bathing" to clean off external parasites. It should not be confused with the *house wren* which is smaller and has a slender bill as well as a tail that often cocks up over its back.

• The robin-sized *mockingbird*, one of the garden's most versatile songsters, may be confused with the *catbird* which is smaller, darker, slimmer, and intersperses its song with telltale mews. The even smaller *junco* which visits us in the winter is darker grey but has a white belly and white outer tail feathers.

• The *chickadee* is hard to miss because of its precise way of articulating its own name. But it does act something like the *tufted titmouse* (the only small grey bird in your garden with a crest) and the *nuthatch* which has the very distinctive habit of climbing down trees headfirst.

• The *chimney swift* is a soot-colored bird with a stubby tail which sails on wind currents with its long wings held in a stiff crescent. Its look-alikes are the *barn swallow*, which has blue-black upper parts, cinnamon lower parts, and a long forked tail, and the *purple martin*, which is blue-black all over and has a long notched tail. There are, of course, many other look-alikes and possible confusions, but I trust that some of my suggestions will help you straighten them out. Another entertaining way of figuring out who's who in the garden is to recognize the pecking order among birds or other animals. In my garden, the who-pecks-whom system varies slightly from season to season.

Doves are unique among birds for their ability to drink water without raising the head skyward. The nestling mourning dove quenches its thirst by means of its parents' "milk", nutritious secretions from the adult bird's crop.

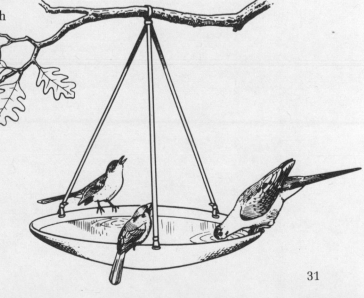

31

I also find that a flock of birds can often scare off a single bird which on a one-to-one basis would have been "king of the feeder." Top bird of the garden social order, winter or summer, is the jaunty blue jay. At bird-bath or feeder he will always be dominant. Although among birds relative size will usually determine who pecks whom, a species with a cocky, aggressive personality, like some sparrows, can pull rank over shyer ones like warblers.

In winter, the evening grosbeak takes second place only to the blue jay, with woodpeckers running a close third. Finches, nuthatches, chickadees, and titmice complete the feeder hierarchy in that order.

In this introduction I have been able to give you only a brief sketch of the fascinating, dynamic world of wildlife. My hope is that you will gain as much enrichment from your garden-watching as I have from mine. And also that you gain a growing awareness of the importance of your individual contribution, as a gardener, as an amateur scientist, and as a generic part of the life process.

Our goal might be to grow personally as one of our great American wildlife watchers grew—Thomas Jefferson, in whose garden notes and letters one may stroll with such pleasure and such a feeling of identification. I remember with particular fondness a letter written from New York in June of 1790, when Jefferson was Secretary of State, to his daughter Polly at Monticello:

> "We had not peas nor strawberries here till the 8th day of this month.
> On the same day I heard the first whip-poor-will whistle. Swallows and martins appeared here on the 21st of April. When did they appear with you? And when had you peas, strawberries, and whip-poor-wills in Virginia? Take notice hereafter whether the whip-poor-wills always come with the strawberries and peas . . ."

Let us indeed always notice hereafter what wildlife appears with the strawberries and peas. It will be good for us.

Mosses (opposite) were among the first plant forms to spread from sea to land as forces mighty as an earthquake and puny as a raindrop slowly ground rock into soil that could at last support life. Sinking rootlets into the meager dirt, mosses became still another soil-maker for the ferns which followed. Today pigeon wheat moss raises spore-filled caps to the wind to sow a new generation in a world where life still depends on soil.

Pigeon Wheat Moss *(Polytrichum sp.)*
by Les Blacklock

32

Gifts of the Soil

Shaggy Mane Mushroom *(Coprinus comatus)* by Grant Heilman

Silver Maple *(Acer saccharinum)* Seedlings by Robert S. Nelson

The Secret of Earth's Bounty— New Life from Old

Inside a pine cone waits a forest. Each seed contains a tree with embryonic root, stem, and needles. Dropping to earth, it pushes down its root, rears upright, and casts aside its shielding husk. Likewise the silver maple seed makes its erratic descent and, taking a grip on soil, begins its climb. From sun and soil the shoots draw energy and nutriment, growing by a secret sorcery called photosynthesis.

As each seed's husk must one day drop, so each life must one day end. What then happens to the husk, the fallen leaf, the toppled tree, the animal that slumps to earth in death? Without decomposition by microbes and the saprophytes that sprout on the residue of death, life itself would smother in its own fallen forms.

The mushroom, appearing overnight as if by elfin magic, is only the spore-bearing fruit of a sprawling underground web of tendrils that can live for centuries. Waiting out dry spells and winters in dormancy, the shaggy mane mushroom wakes to the proper combination of warmth and moisture. Creeping up through rotting log or leaf, the tendrils ooze digestive juices, dissolving the dead matter into a rich broth of nutrients which the tendrils then retrieve. By such unseen chemistry the sturdy maple and the resinous pine surrendered their borrowed bulk to the constant recycling of the soil.

Pine Seedlings by Hugo Skrastins

Our Heroes, the Worm and the Ant

Soil, with its incredible myriads of bacteria and its endless miles of plant roots, must have air and water or all life in it ceases. Hardworking heroes like the ant and the worm make holes in the surface and tunnel beneath to keep the soil a ventilated sponge. Water and air seep down to thirsty roots, and plants above repay the ant with grain for the harvester's underground larders, a dandelion seed for a diligent forager, or nectar that specialized "replete" ants store in swollen bellies and feed to their hungry nestmates.

The earthworm relishes the soil's gift of dead plants and insects, and repays with its castings; these rich fecal nuggets and the worm's constant aerating action can speed by tenfold the building of topsoil.

Harvester Ant *(Pogonomyrmex sp.)* by Ross E. Hutchins

36

Earthworm *(Lumbricus terrestris)* by Alvin E. Staffan

Honey Ant *(Myrmecocystus sp.)* by Paul Wm. Nesbit
Harvester Ant by Ross E. Hutchins

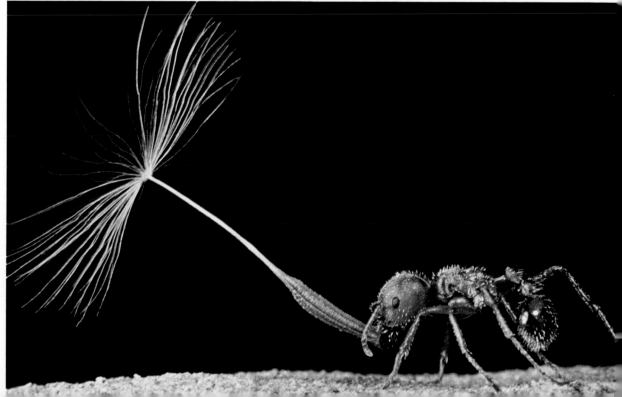

Life and Death on a Blade of Grass

Pathos, humor, lightning-fast action, new life, sudden death—for an exciting afternoon, watch a praying mantis. Tiger of the insect world, this voracious hunter folds its papery wings to prowl on stem and leaf for a beetle or grasshopper, or waits by a blossom to ambush a butterfly or bee. Swaying on four gawky legs, folding two as if to pray, it pounces. Barbed forelegs pin the catch as the mantis eats all but wings and legs, then washes up like a well-fed cat.

Born green amid new spring shoots but grown to brownish old age by fall, the mantis measures four inches at mating time. Then death draws near for the female who lays her eggs in a sac of quick-drying foam—and it's often imminent for the incautious male whose praying won't loosen the grip of his preying paramour.

Female Praying Mantis with egg sac by Eileen Tanson/Tom Stack & Associates

Praying Mantis *(Tenodera sp.)* Nymph by Michael Godfrey

Praying Mantis *(Polyspilota sp.)* by PHOTRI/L. Ingles

White-lipped Snail *(Triodopsis albolabris)* by Larry West

European Garden Snail *(Helix aspersa)* by Lois Cox

Crab Spider *(Misumena sp.)* and
Bumblebee *(Bombus sp.)* by Robert L. Dunne

Following Snail Trails and Spider Webs

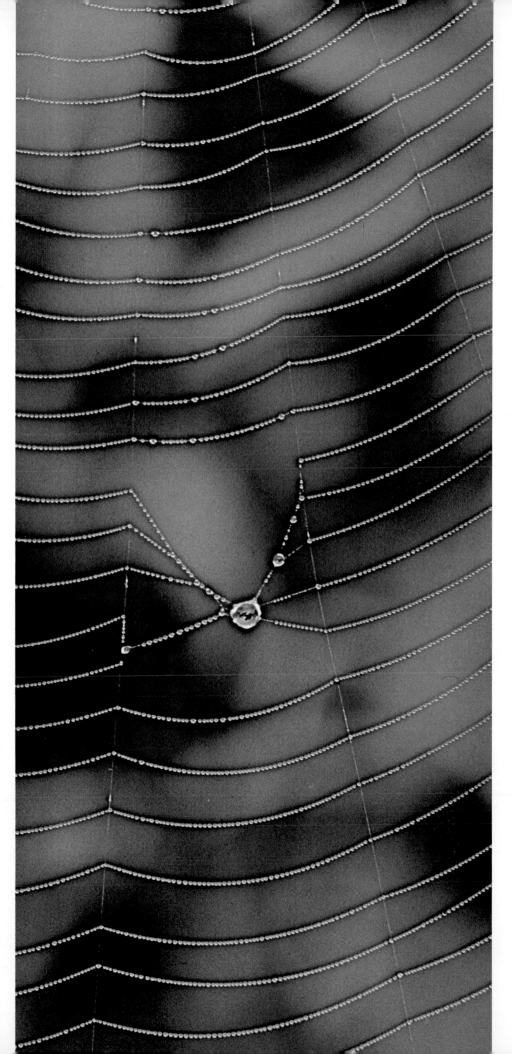

Diamonds of dew on an orb spider's web converge on a scene of death. Here an insect flew into the snare, tangling in sticky cross-strands as its captor raced along the web's dry radial lines to a succulent meal. No web aids the crab spider; by stealth and speed it dooms the agile bee.

Indians revered the spider, for legend says it taught their ancestors to weave. But many shun this shy benefactor whose appetite helps keep pests in check. Leggy, hairy, and sometimes poisonous, it has frightened Miss Muffets on every page of human history.

The slowness of snails amuses us, but we find their feats of strength astonishing. Mostly muscle, a snail can pull nearly 200 times its own weight—like a 10-pound baby towing an automobile. Many snails also lend a hand—or foot, for that is where the raspy mouth is—in nature's clean-up drive. Nevertheless, the pearl-like eggs of Helix aspersa will hatch stalk-eyed slowpokes that can ruin a California lettuce field.

Orb Web by John Shaw

41

Ladybug, Ladybug, Save My Garden!

This polka-dotted pesticide is hatched hungry and stays that way for life. Wiggling out of its tiny yellow egg attached to the underside of a new spring leaf, the ladybug larva heads for the nearest aphid; finding none, it eats its brother. In two to five weeks it grows to nearly half an inch and sports a jaunty jacket of orange and black. Then it pupates, changing its skin for a golden shell and then the shell for crimson armor. Under the armor wait the wings that can lift the ladybug a mile above the earth.

Thus by metamorphosis insects switch from niche to niche—one of the reasons they survive and will probably continue to adapt so well to changes in their environment that they may yet outlive us all.

Ladybug Eggs

Hatching Larvae

Larva

Pupa

Adult

Photos by Eileen Tanson/Tom Stack & Associates

42

Ladybug *(Hippodamia convergens)* by Edward S. Ross

Monarch Butterfly *(Danaus plexippus)* by Edward S. Ross

Honey Bee *(Apis mellifera)* by Larry West

Leonard's Skipper *(Hesperia leonardus)* by Larry West

Wings Among the Blossoms

Insects were the first of nature's creatures to fly. Supremely untouchable, they soared above the plodding predators of earth for many millions of years. Today they soar above the scientist, sometimes confounding his schemes to learn their ways. None can say why the monarch butterfly migrates in flocks for thousands of miles while other kinds hibernate or winter over as larvae or pupae. But we flock to their resting trees to see the sight as they alight and take off in fluttering clouds of dazzling hues.

We glory in the loners, too, watching for a Leonard's skipper to dab its russet on a blazing star. The skipper sails away with beauty in its wake, for, like the honeybee, it pollenates the blossoms as it loots their nectar pots, thus assuring fruit, seed, and bloom to come.

And from the bee we draw the sweet dividend of honey—the nectar of 2,000 flowers in a spoonful—a bonus paid in liquid gold to the prudent gardener who maintains a hive.

Spring Azure (*Celastrina argiolus*)

A Calendar of Butterflies

Great Spangled Fritillary (*Speyeria cybele*)

Know your butterflies, and you can read the rhythm of the seasons as they appear and vanish. One kind flecks your yard with its colors for only a few days, another for several weeks. But early or late on nature's program, each species has its hour onstage. April showers bring spring azures in a flutter of powder blue. By June the lawns and meadows sparkle with the great spangled fritillary and others in a crescendo of colors. August awakens the sleepy orange, often seen clustering by the hundred on a damp spot in a mystifying butterfly ritual called mudding.

Summer ends with a blazing question mark; will this orange-robed hibernator survive the bitter cold ahead? Next September its offspring will flutter their colors on a goldenrod and pose the old question anew.

Sleepy Orange (*Eurema nicippe*)

Question Mark *(Polygonia interrogationis)* Photos by Larry West

2 | Planting an Oasis for Wildlife

By George Reiger

Crisis! What started as a modest invasion of looper caterpillars in the ancient white ash tree by the kitchen door soon took on the proportions of a plague. I had never seen so many inchworms in my life! As they steadily ate their way through the outer fringe of leaves and started on the arboreal equivalent of a crewcut, my wife and I actually whispered the dreaded question: "Should we spray?"

It wasn't only our fear that using the wrong kind of chemical poison would have adverse side effects which caused indecision, it was also our knowledge that, given the gigantic dimensions of the old ash, we'd have to call in a professional team of sprayers with all the attendant high costs. However, just as the scales of judgment were tilting in favor of bringing on the technicians, something quite miraculous (at least as far as we were concerned) happened.

Unknown to us, a mockingbird had set up housekeeping in a lilac bush around the corner of the house from the ash tree, and her young had just hatched. Suddenly we became aware of a great deal of bird activity in the ash. From dawn to dusk the mockingbird flew back and forth between her nest and the tree, returning to her fledglings with two, three, and even four looper caterpillars gripped in her bill. Other birds joined the mockingbird and, within a week, the crisis had abated. In fact, within two weeks, the birds had apparently done such an effective job that they were forced to find happier hunting grounds elsewhere.

For all we knew, the birds may have had some help from yet another of nature's balancing acts, but we were well content with the results. Total cost: nothing. If there had ever been any doubt in our minds about the value of having birds nest around the house, they were forever dispelled by the happy outcome of the great looper crisis.

The springtime garden (opposite) provides with beauty and casual grace all the amenities of good backyard wildlife habitat. With berry-bearing tree and shrub, inviting tangle of hedge and vine, den tree and rocky nook, and— always—water, a well planted hillside becomes an inviting oasis for man and wildlife.
Photo by Paul Genereux

49

A cottontail needs dense cover for daytime protection and winter survival; brood nests, dug out by the female and lined with her fur, are found in open areas of tall grass.

The bluegill sunfish, an important food for bass, is easily spotted at the pond's edge where the male guards the eggs in a shallow nest until they hatch.

Wildlife In the City

Actually, my wife and I have always welcomed all forms of native wildlife to our yard. Enjoying birds, mammals, reptiles, and amphibians as a normal part of daily life even in the city is a legacy of my childhood in Queens County. Although Queens was even in the 1940's one of the five boroughs of New York City, a remarkable assortment of wild creatures visited our half-acre lot on the corner of Puritan Avenue and Greenway South.

One spring I spent hours at the sun parlor window watching an ovenbird build its nest beneath a rhododendron bush. Sitting fascinated like a sidewalk superintendent watching larger construction work go on, I was startled by a movement under a nearby shrub. Petrified that a neighbor's cat had discovered the ovenbird nest, my first reaction was fear. Then a few hops brought a cottontail rabbit within a yard of the ovenbird's nest, and as it sat up to groom the fur on its face, I was enthralled! Should I dash around the house alerting everyone to come and see the rabbit and ovenbird together, or should I sit and enjoy the spectacle all by myself? I decided on the selfish course.

In years following, while my younger brother, John, specialized in cocoon collecting and raising cecropia, promethea, and polyphemus moths, I collected the fascinating array of beetles found in our garden plants, lawn, and hedges. We sometimes combined forces for expeditions to Forest Park and Flushing Meadow, and returned with baby perch and bluegills for our aquarium and garter snakes and frogs for our terrarium.

We fed the birds in our yard from a simple covered platform atop an upright iron pipe. While squirrels, opossums, and raccoons could never actually get into the feeder or molest the birds because of the intervening metal pole, we often found their tracks on the ground or snow around the base of the feeder. Actually the squirrels weren't as interested in the birds as they were in the nuts and seeds we put out for them. But since birds are restless, rambunctious eaters, they frequently scattered enough from the tray to feed up to two and three squirrels at a time sitting below the station, picking up and using what the birds appeared to discard.

Guests Can Become Pests

Although John and I reveled in the antics of these four-footed freeloaders, we soon learned that to home-owning parents, squirrels are a mixed blessing. Given an inch, they, and raccoons, too, often take a mile. In fact, one summer we received stern orders to discourage the squirrels around the feeder after we discovered a whole family of them living in the attic!

To this day, my brothers and I marvel at how calmly our mother responded to our rather hysterical announcement that there were squirrels residing over Johnny's room. Reared in the Virginia countryside, she soon had the squirrel invasion under control. Unknown to us, Mom was an old hand at making box traps. She quickly made a pattern for the trap, went out and bought the plywood and other materials she'd need, and then assembled the contraption with the few tools we had in the basement. She set the trap, caught the squirrels, and then loaded the captives and us into the car for a long drive to the middle of Long Island where the animals were safely released in a large woodlot. Cooking and housecleaning we took for granted—but imagine having a real live mother who could trap squirrels! We boasted about her achievement all over school, much to her embarrassment at parent-teacher meetings.

The Secret of Attracting Wildlife

Of course it was the big old oaks along the streets, far more than the overflow from our bird feeder, which attracted squirrels to our home in Queens, and it was the lilac bush which caught the eye of the mockingbird when she, in a nest-building mood, made her first reconnaissance flight around our neighborhood in Virginia. So if you would like to see more birds and mammals in your yard, consider the trees and shrubs you are offering them. Flowers have a role, too, and of course there must be water, but choice and location of trees and shrubs are basic.

If creating a mini-refuge around your home is your goal, we are glad to share our discoveries with you, pausing only long enough for a "Welcome to the club!" handshake and a warning that you are entering into a new relationship with nature that can absorb and enrich the rest of your life. It could even change your whole life-style.

How big is your yard? How many and what kinds of plantings do you have on hand? And how do you want to improve the situation? What native wildlife species can you reasonably hope to attract? Before going any further with specifics, let's look at a model backyard plan (pp. 52-53), one that was drawn up by a team of landscape architects and wildlife biologists working at the U.S. Forest Service Environmental Forestry Research Unit in Amherst, Massachusetts. Their goal was to create a wildlife habitat which would be esthetically pleasing to people. While the team selected plants which grow well in the Northeast, their plan can be adapted to any part of the country.

These experts started with nothing more than a quarter-acre sodded yard like that found around a development home. Even if your yard is smaller, consider their choices of plantings because every tree, shrub, and flower was selected for its capacity to attract wildlife. The plan is shown in three stages so no matter whether your yard is old or new, you may be able to utilize some of their ideas.

Live-trapping is the most humane way to control problem animals. To prevent unnecessary suffering, the trap must be lined with nesting material and checked twice daily.

Stage I First-year planting of model backyard wildlife habitat. Shrubs are low, trees appear scattered.

Stage II (Below) After five to ten years' growth, shrubs nearly full size, trees up to 25 feet high.

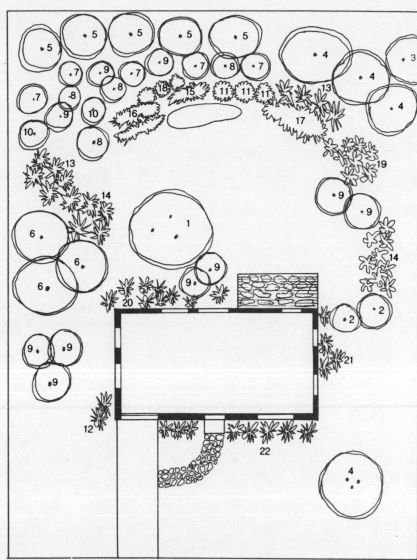

Backyard Wildlife Habitat Planting Plan

Stage I (upper left) shows the new plantings as viewed from the terrace at the rear of the house. With birds the principal visitors, feeding stations are set up to supplement the fruits on the young trees and shrubs. A birdbath provides water.

Stage II (lower left) depicts the transformation wrought by five to ten years' growth and the replacement of the birdbath with a small pool. The number of birds has increased, but food on the bough has eliminated need for feeders.

Numbers in the planting diagram (above) of the 100' x 120' backyard are keyed to the following species:

Large Trees—*(1) beech; (2) holly; (3) white oak; (4) red maple; (5) white pine; (6) white spruce; (7) hemlock.* **Small Trees**—*(8) mountain ash; (9) flowering dogwood; (10) crabapple.* **Large Shrubs**—*(11) winterberry; (12) downy serviceberry; (13) autumn olive; (14) viburnum; (15) elderberry.* **Small Shrubs**—*(16) blackberry; (17) silky dogwood; (18) red osier dogwood; (19) Tartarian honeysuckle; (20) snowberry; (21) Japanese barberry; (22) rhododendron or other ornamental suitable to site.* **Flowers** *for planters and scattered beds— asters, daisies, marigolds, petunias, black-eyed Susans, sunflowers.*

Stage III After 30 to 40 years' growth. Trees and shrubs at full maturity create massed clumps of vegetation.

Since the first year's plantings in the model yard could do little more than indicate the good things to come, the professionals relied on the owner to supply artificial feeders and water from some source. Thus they provided as many of the essentials as possible from the start. And even at that early stage, the wildlife population begins to build. Flowers attract butterflies and other insects which in turn attract birds. Robins feed on the lawn while sparrows and finches may forage among the new shrubs. You may even see an occasional cottontail.

Five to ten years into the project (Stage II), most shrubs are full grown, trees are 25 feet high and already beginning to screen out views of the neighbors' bicycle and lawn mower collection and the shouts of their children. The addition of a small pool gives the garden a new center of interest for both birds and mammals drawn by the glint of water; it also creates its

own aquatic community of plants and insects which attract small reptiles and amphibians. Cardinals and catbirds should be joining the robins and sparrows nesting in shrubbery which is now dense enough at ground level to provide cover for rabbits and chipmunks.

Stage III represents not only the culmination of effort, but the fulfillment of a lifetime dream. While a variety of birds nest in the mature trees, the dense understory of shrubs provides escape routes for small birds and mammals chased by the fat tomcat and the bumbling beagle from down the block. Besides creating a backyard of enormous beauty which brings elements of the wilderness into the city, the owner has created a wildlife oasis with economic as well as esthetic values. For whether you eventually sell your house or keep it for family reunions, a well-designed backyard habitat for wildlife is money invested, not merely spent.

Stage III is a fruitful, self-renewing backyard habitat at the height of its capacity to attract wildlife. Chickadees, siskins, and crossbills feed and nest in tall conifers; tanagers, warblers, and orioles live in the tops of the hardwoods, while squirrels and raccoons den in their hollows. Rabbits feed on the lawn while garter snakes, frogs, and dragonflies are drawn to the pool. From chipmunks to butterflies, it's the sort of home which wildlife is looking for.

You Start With a Plan

Now to design your own backyard refuge. Whatever its present stage of development, and whether you decide to adapt the model to your property or try a different approach, the immediate steps are the same.

(1) Take a piece of graph paper and do a scaled diagram of all your property's dimensions. Include the house, walkways, and other permanent constructions, but exclude current plantings. Make several copies.

(2) Fill in one copy with your current plantings, down to the types and precise locations of flowers in each bed and the kinds of grasses in the lawn. This is your "before" record. It will be helpful later on in determining where you may want to move plants already in the ground as well as where to plant new things.

(3) Now comes the fun part—the dream. Don't rush it. Start by gathering all the information you can. Make notes on ideas which appeal to you as you read this book. Even if you continue through all the titles recommended in the bibliography (see page 186—Ed.), there are many other valuable sources to tap. They will acquaint you not only with the many possibilities open to you, but with the probable costs in time, energy, and money.

There Are Habitats for Any Budget

The beauty of landscaping your backyard for wildlife is that you have a choice between getting gradual results with occasional investments of little time and little money, or dramatically improving your backyard habitat in a show of conspicuous consumption that will dazzle your neighbors. Done wisely as well as thriftily or lavishly, wildlife won't care whether you did it yourself in a decade or hired a landscape architect to do it in a season. Because of a more limited budget, and because I dislike turning any form of recreation into a project, I lean toward modest changes and improvements in a landscape on a long-term basis.

For example, I don't rush to the nearest nursery to buy each new shrub and tree I need. I wait for my next invitation to the home of friends or relatives in the country and ask them to let me visit their woodlot. Since I'm something of a snob about exotics and prefer native American trees and shrubs, I keep my country friends—and my neighbors, also—alerted to my planting needs for laurel, bayberry, birch, beech, and dogwood. They let me know their needs, too, and when I see a shrub that would fit into one of the gaps in our hedge, or a young tree that is needed in the northwest corner of the backyard, often we can arrange a profitable swap. Roadside specimens are also tempting, but many states have laws against removing them—even for the high purpose of serving wildlife better in a backyard setting!

A wild sapling is easier to identify after it has leafed out, but transplanting it is risky at this stage. Either return for the plant in the fall or be sure you remove a big ball of dirt with the roots as you dig it up.

A safer plan is to watch for surveyors' flags going up on the site of a new shopping mall or road construction, and get in touch with the owner. Since he's probably going to pay to have most of the plantings gouged out anyway, you may get some nice stock. To be prepared for such opportunities, I keep a collapsible trenching shovel and a sheet of plastic in the back of my car with which to wrap the ball of earth that should come with the plant. But even if the roots come away without any earth, I wrap the bottom of the plant in plastic after, if possible, saturating the roots in water. Using such primitive transplanting methods, I've kept plants alive and well in the trunk during cool weather for many days and had them thrive when planted later at home.

For best results, these young saplings taken from the wild should not be more than two or three feet high.

If you're willing to start with tree and shrub seedlings, check with your state's Division of Forestry. Some states provide certain species of wild-life-attracting plants such as autumn olive at well below nursery cost. Although the minimum order may include more seedlings than you personally have room for, your neighbors or garden club members may be able to share them in a community planting project. You must, however, explain to the forester in the local office exactly how and where you plan to use the plants in order to be approved as a purchaser.

A nursery's most popular and best-advertised trees and shrubs may be of little value to birds and other animals. Ask your nurseryman to show you the many viburnums, hollies, dogwoods, and other species which can make your yard distinctive as well as inviting to wildlife.

Visit Local Nurseries

Of course nursery stock seems expensive compared with saplings given to you by friendly landowners or seedlings purchased from the state, but for some varieties and in some circumstances, you have no choice. But then, nursery plants are always balled in good soil and usually guaranteed for a year after purchase. Some nurseries will also deliver stock and even plant it without additional charge if your order is large enough. Nurseries are also infinitely more productive of the ideal specimens you want than looking around the countryside for wild ones. So talk to nurserymen. Regard their working knowledge of horticulture and landscaping in your community as one of your legitimate sources of information. Describe your goals and get their suggestions for attaining them. See what plants they feature, looking especially for those that will provide food and shelter for wildlife. If you don't see what you want, ask if they can order it for you. Follow their directions for caring for the stock you do buy.

Still another gold mine of information are the successful wildlife gardeners in your neighborhood. Don't be shy about asking how they achieved specific results. They're usually most happy to discuss why their gardens attract so many cardinals or how they feed their dogwoods. Chances are, they'll share some wonderful nuggets of wisdom such as a warning not to plant red cedar with crabapple trees because the cedar is an alternate host to a rust which spots crabapple leaves and fruit. It was from just such an over-the-fence visit that we learned to propagate willow trees by clipping the end of a branch and sticking it in the ground, and that you can start pin oaks by planting acorns in a flower pot on the window sill.

Know Your Soil

While altitude and climate zone play important roles in determining the kinds of flora you can grow, soil type is extremely important and, unlike the other two variables, you can do something about it. The first step is to have the soil analyzed for its present content of such vital elements as nitrogen, phosphorus, and potassium. If you're having difficulties getting some of your favorite trees or shrubs to grow, and lime and fertilizers don't solve the problem, it's often possible to substitute plants that will thrive in your soil. A chemical soil analysis is the key.

Your best bet for a reliable and usually free soil test is to contact your county agricultural agent. You'll find his office listed in the telephone book under the name of your county. Look under "Cooperative Extension Service." In any event, don't keep trying to plant something in an area where it clearly doesn't want to grow. Once your soil is analyzed you will probably know the reason why. I once ignored my own advice and spent two springs trying to get multiflora rose to grow where the ground was still too salty following some excavation work. Had I taken a soil sample to the county agent at the outset, I would have discovered that bayberry was a much more suitable choice for that particular location than multiflora rose.

A spadeful of soil wriggling with earthworms assures the gardener of good vegetable crops and vigorous trees and shrubs. Good soil is home and larder to countless other creatures such as the beetle larva which becomes food for burrowing turtle, toad, and eft. These in turn enrich the soil with fecal droppings and aerate it with tunnels dug in search of coolness and moisture. The eyed elater beetle joins other insects in honeycombing a rotting log into a form the scavenging snail can recycle into fertile topsoil.

Eyed elater

Beetle larva

Land snails

American toad

Red eft

Box turtle

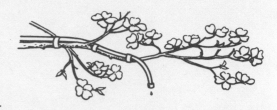

Don't Forget Water

While a great diversity of plantings will provide food, cover and reproductive sites, all wildlife needs water as well. You can't leave it to the rain collected in hollows at the base of tree limbs to answer all the birds' water needs, nor expect lawn sprinkler runoff to take care of the year-round needs of squirrels, chipmunks, and rabbits. Birds are more likely to come to a birdbath which is well off the ground with clear visibility all around so that no predators can sneak up while they're playing in the water. Most mammals look for a ground-level water source. Since pools, fountains, and birdbaths also tend to become esthetic focal points in the backyard design, it's doubly important to decide on your habitat's chief water source or sources early in the planning stage. Even if you have to make do with a pan of water on the portable barbecue temporarily, you can at least place the barbecue on the site of the future pool and get the plantings started around it. A seasonal succession of flowers can vary the birdbath scene.

A birdbath, whether it serves as a temporary or permanent substitute for a garden pool, can be enhanced by landscaping around it. You can add sound and motion to the watering spot, increasing its attraction for birds, by attaching a dripping hose along an overhanging branch.

Don't Overdo It

When your first new shrubs and trees begin to improve on the sparse foundation plantings and the single tree dropped into place by your developer as token landscaping, it's easy to get carried away. In a few years you can create such a jungle of shrubbery everywhere on the property as to exclude robins and other species of wildlife that need and enjoy a little lawn space.

By succumbing to that great American maxim that anything worth doing is worth overdoing, you can also rob yourself of adequate vistas for viewing wildlife without disturbing it. While it may be hard to believe now, even the six- and eight-inch seedlings you have just put in the ground have the capacity to reach full flowering shrub or tree dimensions within five to 25 years. So it isn't enough to plant holly trees indiscriminately just because birds like the berries. The hollies must have a specific role in your overall plan, they must be the kind of holly which can best fulfill that role, and they must be properly located. If you want to treat the holly as specimens, plan, plant, and prune them accordingly (not overlooking the fact that you will need both a male and a female plant). But if you prefer holly to be a part of a hedge, a different set of rules must be drawn up at the outset. We'll get to hedges in a moment.

Know Your Limitations

Try as you will, there's simply no way to recreate the Rocky Mountain ecosystem of your childhood in an Indiana suburb. Don't try to plant palm trees in Virginia (yes, I know a few have made it) or duplicate your neighbor's bald cypress in Wisconsin (with constant care and luck, anything's

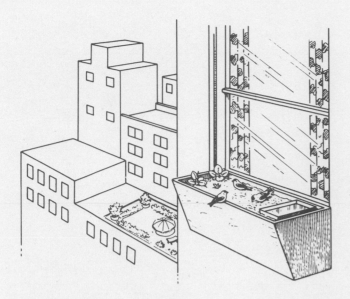

Roof gardens and even high-rise window boxes are sometimes visited by night-flying migrants. Lured by city lights, these small birds come down to rest and feed. In rural areas they keep moving from grove to grove, but in city parks, hemmed in by tall buildings, they stay for a day or two, giving urban bird-watchers a rare opportunity.

possible). Your wildlife habitat is meant to be an oasis for you as well as for wildlife, and anything requiring constant attention is simply not in the spirit of creating a mini-refuge for wildlife.

If you live on the inner fringe of the suburbs, you expect to have more bird visitors than someone living downtown, but fewer than someone living in the country. By the same token, if you are limited to a flower box on an apartment windowsill, you accept the fact that a ground floor box with food and water, or one located on a window at treetop level, will attract more birds than a box feeder located far above the urban tree line. If you live high up and in the heart of a vertical world like New York City, well, count your blessings if you see a rock dove—alias common pigeon—every now and then. But even here, if you have windows that open and a window box or tray which can be securely installed from inside, with a little greenery and color in the flowers, a dish of seeds, and a cup of water, the incredible can occur.

I recall a lady neighbor living on the 14th floor of a Manhattan apartment building who had a window box overlooking a rooftop garden some six stories below with a number of backyard gardens some eight stories below that. Our neighbor had high hopes when she planted her box in midwinter but when, week after week, nothing appeared, she became discouraged. Periodically she emptied and refilled the seed and water dishes because they became coated with soot and grime. She resolved to stick with her plan for a 14th-floor oasis until she went through the one bag of mixed bird seed she had purchased before Christmas.

Then one cold April day, she came hammering on our apartment door, shouting as if to arouse every tenant in the building. She wanted me to come quick to see the "canaries" at her feeder. Dubious but extremely curious, I rushed back with her to see what she had. Lo and behold, like something out of a dream, there were three goldfinches hopping about her burgeoning flower garden in miniature, eating and scattering seeds and having a splashing good time in the bath. I was amazed, but my neighbor took it all in stride: "I suppose because they're so pretty," she said, "they think they don't have to have good manners!"

While birds like warblers and finches do show up in Manhattan during migrations, and even robins, cardinals, and flickers will nest in Central Park, the closer you live to significant green space, the greater your odds of having not only significant numbers of visitors to your wildlife habitat, but satisfying variety, too. A few birds have adapted astonishingly well to life in the concrete canyons, but the dearth of green in the city explains why you usually see only starlings, sparrows, and pigeons there.

Backyard Habitat Study

In 1973 Curt Jansen, a student in the Department of Fishery and Wildlife Biology at Colorado State University, developed a questionnaire for bird-watchers to find whether there were specific habitat characteristics which encouraged a rich and varied birdlife in the suburban areas of Ft. Collins, Colorado. He found that neighborhoods with high floral diversity, including numerous trees and shrubs of various heights, many species of trees and shrubs, a source of water, and open space in the form of a park or undeveloped land, had a correspondingly high abundance and variety of birdlife. For example, people living in neighborhoods with the five highest habitat-diversity ratings reported seeing between 30 and 183 species of birds, while people living in the five lowest habitat-diversity neighborhoods never saw more than 20 species. Equally significant, the higher the habitat diversity, the more sightings reported of many individuals of all species. By comparison, more single bird sightings per species were reported in the low habitat-diversity areas.

Variety is the Key

Clearly, one of the most significant and immediate contributions you can make to the bird welfare of your backyard is to imitate the Forest Service's model plan in providing as much variety in your plantings as possible—even if you can't attain its totals of ten species of trees and 12 shrub species.

Establishing a hedge along one side of your property is an ideal way to do this. A hedge made up of only four species—American holly, privet, autumn olive, and serviceberry—will provide food most of the year. Your bird visitors, attracted by the blackish pome of the serviceberry in July, will not have to move elsewhere for food as summer wanes; for the red berries of the holly start ripening in August, followed by the red drupe of

A year-round bird buffet, the hedge below serves (1) elderberries, (2) snowberries, and (3) dogwood from August until the fall ripening of (4) autumn olive, (5) viburnums, and (6) winterberry which last into the colder months. (7) Sumacs provide important winter sustenance as do the festive (8) holly and the September-to-May fruit of the (9) red cedar. Beneficial to people as well as to wildlife, a varied hedge provides privacy, a windbreak, and splashes of seasonal color in leaf and fruit.

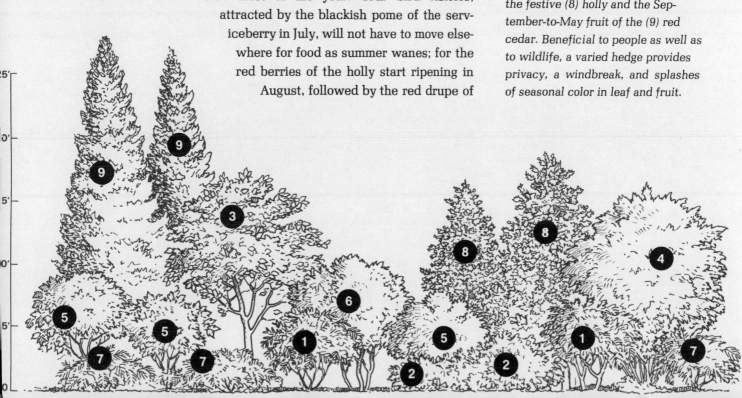

Tall trees that soften or camouflage rooftops will obviously be more appealing as rest stops to weary migrant birds than a new development outlined by the hard lines of new roadways and barren expanses of lawn. The birdwatcher's chances of seeing an unusual visitor along the flyway are directly related to the size and quantity of neighborhood greenery.

the autumn olive and the black berry of the privet in September and October. Supplemented by cut fruit and seeds in one or more feeders, these natural foods will nourish a veritable army of birds all winter long. Besides providing nesting sites and protection against inclement weather and predators, a hedge also provides food and cover for small mammals—altogether, a far greater contribution to wildlife habitat for the effort expended than that required for an open lawn.

If you already have some useful shrubs on the property, so much the better. Some home owners enjoy moving their smaller plantings every year or so, about the same time and for the same obscure reason the lady of the house rearranges the living room furniture. Perhaps you've grown tired of lilacs or found that lilac shrubs are relatively low in bird food value. But if you are a compulsive plant rearranger, don't throw away the old shrubs. A combination hedge is an ideal destiny for those which have fallen from favor, and even a lilac bush makes a good home for a mockingbird family.

If you simply have too many shrubs for one hedge, then by all means start another—or ring neighbors' doorbells and ask them if they'd like to have some of your surplus for their garden. Remember, the more home owners in your neighborhood who birdscape their yards, the more wildlife will be attracted to the area for everyone's benefit and pleasure.

Tall Trees Are Important

While clusters and hedges of shrubs are the key to the greatest diversity for backyard wildlife, the value of tall trees cannot be overlooked. Fortunately, increasing numbers of developers—either out of conscience or because of new ordinances—are leaving many of the trees originally found growing on undeveloped wooded lots. Common practice once included selling the prospective homeowner an attractive piece of land whose title included ownership of the topsoil and all flora. Then while the new and inexperienced landowner wasn't looking, the developer would come in, cut down all the trees (insisting they were too hard or dangerous to work around while constructing the house), sell the trees to a pulp mill or firewood distributor, and then scrape off the topsoil and sell that to a nursery or another landowner who had previously lost his topsoil! It was (and in some areas still is) a ghastly game which left the new homeowner poorer and a little more cynical, and left his former bird residents without any place to feed, rest, or hide.

Significantly, in Curt Jansen's studies at Colorado State University, there is one criterion that was closely related to the number of birds seen— namely the age of the neighborhood: the older the residential area, the more tall trees, the more birds seen.

Besides acting as magnets for migrant birds, tall trees also provide permanent homes to birds that do not rest or nest in hedges. Still other bird species need the cavities found only in older trees for nesting holes. For example, if there are no mature trees on your property or in the neighborborhood, you simply won't see many woodpeckers. And orioles rarely nest close to the ground. In fact, in many parts of our country, their beautifully-woven baskets were intimately associated with the giant elms that once graced so many towns and city streets. Today, with Dutch elm disease having led to the loss of a majority of these stately trees, and with municipalities slow to replace them with trees of equal size and value, the oriole has disappeared from many areas of former abundance.

Yet there's no shortcut to the growth of tall, substantial trees. Worse, not everyone recognizes their value. In some communities, definite obstacles have been put in the way of friends who were trying to grow them and other wildlife-serving vegetation. Our friends have actually been threatened with legal action for cultivating trees allegedly hazardous to the roofs and gables of neighboring homes. Patient explanations of what you are trying to do, careful pruning of any dead or dying branches that may actually pose a threat to a neighbor's welfare, and possibly even an appeal to their more venal natures by pointing out that homes with many tall trees are always worth more than homes with none, are the only appropriate responses to make to such persons. And there is always the hope that one may in the long run even convert a few.

Choosing Your Plantings

As various elements of your dream plan crystallize in your mind, the lists of plantings on page 65 should be helpful in making final choices. To adapt the model plan (pages 52-55) drawn up for the northeastern part of the country by the U.S. Forest Service team, simply check the lists for your part of the country. Each tree, shrub, vine, grass, and flower is highly recommended for its capacity to supply food and/or cover for one or more species of wildlife. Of course they represent just a handful of the many possibilities, and certainly some species listed for the region might be successfully grown in others. Generally, however, we can guarantee that where these

The downy woodpecker feeds in the bark of old trees on ants, weevils, and caterpillars. It drills out an 8- to 12-inch cavity in a dead tree or branch in which to nest, but sometimes accepts a log birdhouse.

Palmetto fruit is an important food for Florida's robins and raccoons. The brown-headed nuthatch depends on the indigenous pines for more than half its diet. Retaining (or re-establishing) native flora is the surest way of keeping native fauna in a developing area.

plants grow, wildlife will be found.

As you begin to work with the scale drawing of your yard, you will need additional information about each plant—its height at maturity; when it flowers and when the fruit ripens; whether it grows well in sun or shade, and in wet or dry conditions; and which species of wildlife it serves in what ways. These facts are provided in the Appendix (pages 177-183) for the plants and trees listed on the facing page. One word of caution: while the lists of plantings provide choices for each region, there are unique zones where climate or soil extremes may narrow those choices and even frustrate you into enlisting the assistance of local gardening experts. The remedy may lie in sticking to fewer, but tried-and-true, native plants.

In southern Florida, for instance, warm winters permit the successful growth of a number of outdoor tropical plants. However, since my plea is always on behalf of local flora anyway, I'd like to persuade more Floridians to re-establish the slash pine and palmetto margins which their developer replaced with exotic stands of punk-trees *(Melaleuca leucadendron)* and Brazilian pepper *(Schinus terebinthifolius).* For the same reason, on sand dunes or offshore barrier islands, native pine, sea grape, and bayberry are more at home and generally more successful than exotic windbreaks of, say, Lombardy poplar *(Populus nigra).*

Wherever you live, keep working through the lists until you arrive at the ideal combination for your soil type, your time schedule, your pocketbook, and for the native birds, mammals, amphibians, reptiles, and insects you may reasonably hope to attract.

That last element—what it is reasonable to hope to attract—is important. While there's no harm in trying to tip the scales a bit in favor of certain preferred guests, not everyone who lives in Maine will want to try to duplicate the experience of Dr. and Mrs. Polydor Komianos who were delighted to discover a regal bull moose browsing on the back lawn of their National Wildlife Backyard Habitat No. 142 near Alna. Nor will all Californians follow the example of Dr. and Mrs. Emilio Marrero whose salt lick has attracted coyotes, deer, and a mountain lion to their two acres of chapparal, Backyard Habitat No. 178, near Malibu. However, Chicago suburbanites might want to emulate the achievement of Art Kozelka, Garden Editor of the *Chicago Tribune,* whose winter feeding program brings dozens of pheasants to his snow-covered backyard, and Southerners may want to plant a yard like Backyard Habitat No. 31, owned by Mr. and Mrs. James D. Lyon of Oak Grove, Louisiana, which attracts pileated woodpeckers, quail, and wood ducks along with rabbits, squirrels, and 27 other species of birds to their one-acre lot.

If you want mammals but don't have enough mature hardwoods for squirrels, and can't bear to share your vegetable garden with rabbits, the chipmunk offers a nice compromise between normal shyness and the nuisance any

Suggested Wildlife Plantings For Your Part Of The Country

FLOWERS & GRASSES	LOW SHRUBS & VINES	LARGE SHRUBS	SMALL TREES	LARGE TREES
Northeast				
Panicgrass	Blackberry	Autumn olive	Cherry	Beech
Sunflower	Spicebush	Dogwood	Crabapple	Birch
Timothy	Snowberry	Elderberry	Dogwood	Colorado spruce
Bristlegrass	Coralberry	Sumac	Hawthorn	Hemlock
Ragweed	Virginia creeper	Winterberry	Red cedar	Sugar maple
Knotweed	Greenbrier	Tartarian honeysuckle	Serviceberry	White oak
Pokeweed	Mapleleaf viburnum	Highbush blueberry	Mulberry	White pine
	Bittersweet	Multiflora rose		Blackgum
	Japanese honeysuckle	Firethorn		Red maple
		Highbush cranberry		Boxelder
Northwest				
Filaree	Blackberry	Elderberry	Dogwood	California black oak
Sunflower	Oregon grape	Sumac	Hawthorn	Colorado spruce
Tarweed	Snowberry	Tartarian honeysuckle	Serviceberry	Douglasfir
Timothy	Coralberry	Multiflora rose		Lodgepole pine
Turkeymullein	Gooseberry	Firethorn		Ponderosa pine
Bristlegrass	Buckthorn	Highbush cranberry		Boxelder
Ragweed	Sagebrush	Russian olive		
Knotweed				
Southeast				
Lespedeza	Bayberry	Dogwood	Cherry	Mountain-ash
Panicgrass	Blackberry	Elderberry	Crabapple	Beech
Sunflower	Spicebush	Sumac	Dogwood	Hackberry
Bristlegrass	Virginia creeper	Tartarian honeysuckle	Hawthorn	Live oak
Ragweed	Greenbrier	Highbush blueberry	Holly	Loblolly pine
Knotweed	Mapleleaf viburnum	Multiflora rose	Palmetto	Pecan
Pokeweed	Japanese honeysuckle	Firethorn	Persimmon	Slash pine
		Arrowwood	Red cedar	Blackgum
			Serviceberry	Red maple
			Mulberry	Boxelder
Southwest				
Filaree	Blackberry	Manzanita	Crabapple	Live oak
Sunflower	Juniper	Sumac	Dogwood	Pin oak
Turkeymullein	Pricklypear	Tartarian honeysuckle	Mesquite	Pinyon pine
Bristlegrass	Virginia creeper	Multiflora rose	Serviceberry	Boxelder
Ragweed	Sagebrush	Firethorn	Mulberry	
Knotweed				

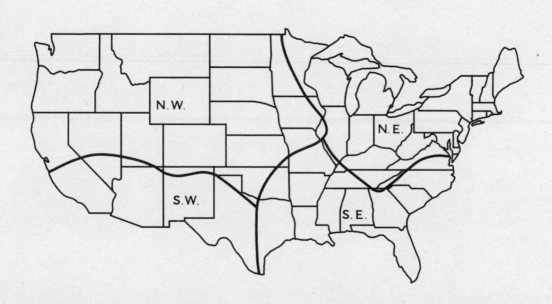

animal may become after overcoming its fear of humans. Clean, neat, and an underground dweller, besides being a connoisseur of cutworms and beetles, the chippie's charming antics more than repay for the nuts, seeds, and fruits it eats. Unlike many rodents and raccoons who will move in with you if given the chance, chipmunks generally stay about the stone walls and roots of old trees where they normally make their home. What you can add is enough ground-covering plants to give them safe travel routes from their burrows to water and food sources.

If stone walls are common in your part of the country, you may find them frequented by an interesting assortment of wildlife other than chipmunks. Indeed, even if stone is rare where you live and you'd like to give lizards, for example, an opportunity to enjoy your backyard habitat, then brick walls constructed with open spaces provide more cover than do solid straight walls.

Wildlife Preferences

As different people prefer different foods, so do different species of wildlife. There's no one plant that serves as the favorite food for all birds and mammals. For example, while many birds enjoy raspberries as a summer fruit, white-tailed deer will eat the stems only as an alternative to starvation in winter. On the other hand, deer love to browse on hemlock, a tree that birds use more for cover than for food.

Each species of wildlife has different dietary needs, and most feeding patterns are a response to the body's call for different minerals, fats, and protein. Contrary to what many people believe, wild creatures are not being shortchanged in their consumption of uncultivated foods. Far from it. According to *American Wildlife and Plants* by Alexander, Zim, and Nelson (a book every wildlife gardener should know), there is only 14 percent protein in the eggs humans eat, 19 percent in our sirloin steak, and 22 percent protein in chicken. By contrast, seeds from black locust, lespedeza, sweet clover, pine, and many others all contain in excess of 25 percent protein. Pork chops and veal offer us respectively 24 percent and 16 percent fat value, while hazelnuts, hickory nuts, and acorns all provide wildlife with more than 25 percent fat. Hackberries have twice the protein of domestic raisins; greenbrier has nine times the sugar value and two times the protein value of spinach; and wild cherries are twice as rich in protein as cultivated sweet cherries. In short, wildlife hardly suffers from malnutrition in consuming native

The white-tailed deer prefers a habitat of cutover timberland because it provides an abundance of low forage around the edges. In winter deer will often bed down under low hanging conifer branches which provide shelter from cold and snow.

fruits, seeds, and nuts! Poor diets are usually the result of unavailability, rather than unsuitability, of wild foods. This most often occurs in the depths of winter when all available food has been eaten or is covered by deep snow or sleet. It's at such times that backyard feeding stations play the life-saving role for which they were designed. By providing a variety of foods in your feeder, you'll be answering the varied dietary needs of a wider spectrum of wildlife in much the same way the naturally produced fruits, nuts, and berries in your mini-refuge feed many different species before the hard lean months of winter set in.

Keeping Wildlife Wild

This business of attracting birds with artificial feeders, even to the point of distracting them from a portion of their wild life-style, by becoming dependent on what you dole out at the food tray, haunts the entire backyard habitat effort. The hummingbird is a case in point.

This feathered jewel is designed for hovering and feeding in tubular flowers. In the East, jewelweed, morning glory, honeysuckle, and cardinal flower are favored plants, while in California and the Southwest, manzanita, yucca, columbine, and evening primrose are visited by hummingbirds. They also respond well to a large number of cultivated flowers, among which are gladiolus, petunias, nasturtiums, begonias, and hibiscus. We have even had hummingbirds drawn to our lilac bush. Such ambivalence about what hummers respond to points up a number of small problems relating to hummingbirds in particular and to your mini-refuge in general.

First of all, contrary to popular belief, hummingbirds do not live on honey water, or even flower nectar. They definitely have a sweet tongue for honey water, especially if served in a bright red feeder or if the liquid is dyed red. But this is saying no more than that children love ice cream. They do. But they'd eventually perish if that was all you fed them.

When hummingbirds pose so delicately before a morning glory and sip deep within its cup, the bird is seeking both nectar and insects. The mother hummer regurgitates this food into the stomachs of her young which need that insect protein to grow on. The hummingbird uses the nectar of flowers and fruit juices as a source of quick energy in order to maintain its furious rate of activity. Plain table sugar and water in bright artificial feeders will attract hummers, but will not provide the immediate charge needed by this little dynamo.

So make sure you have first planted their preferred flowers and shrubs, from which they can attain a balanced diet of insects and nectar. Then, if you wish to use the additional lure of an artificial hummingbird feeder, fill it with honey and water, not sugar water (see page 126—Ed.).

For the same reason, plant the trees and shrubs which will feed all the

Over 300 species of hummingbirds live in the Americas, but only the ruby-throat regularly visits eastern United States. Some 15 other species are found in the Southwest, but it takes binoculars, a quick eye, and a good bird book to tell them apart.

wildlife that visit your backyard insofar as that is possible. If there are gaps in what your backyard plantings provide naturally, try to plan your backyard feeder menu to suppplement these specific deficiencies artificially. But once started, you should only stop by tapering off gradually. And if feeding in the wintertime, you're under a moral obligation to continue until spring.

Don't Expect Too Much

My last warning about your relationship with wildlife is not to be overoptimistic. I know one lady in Florida who has more hibiscus, passion flowers, and honey-water feeders in her garden than anyone for 50 miles around! But she's unhappy because she receives only occasional visits from hummingbirds. They haven't set up housekeeping by the hundreds as she imagined they would when she first started planning and planting.

To a lesser degree, this is the experience of many backyard enthusiasts. They try to remain realistic, but still they expect their garden to attract just a little more wildlife than any other garden in town. The reason one species of bird visits your backyard and not another may be something beyond control, such as location or soil type. Therefore, don't expect every bird in the Peterson Field Guide to show up on your porch, and don't think that because you've built a 6-foot diameter pool that you'll have Canada geese dropping down for a visit. Find happiness in the small wonders that will occur in any mini-refuge and look for serenity in your plantings and in what few creatures visit them. Leave competition at the office or the bridge table.

If You Have More Than One-Fourth Acre

A single season of long, hot Saturday afternoons on a riding mower should be enough to convince you that part of your land might be better off as woods, field, or a pond than as a vast swarth of neatly manicured turf. Not only will you save liters of petroleum and perspiration, but converting part of the lawn to trees and water will mean more wildlife.

Think back on the last time you visited a large country estate or park. Where did you see the most birds or find deer tracks? Not on the sweeping, carpet-like lawns. Oh, they're lovely, all right. But most wildlife is found at the edges of the woods, or around a pool or stream. You may even have discovered a nesting pair of quail in a well-screened flower bed.

The same is true of golf links. A course that eliminates cover provides a limited environment for wildlife and golfer alike. While a few players will curse the course that costs them a large number of lost balls, most golfers derive an esthetic satisfaction beyond the mere mechanics of the game

The elusive wild turkey, benefiting from wise management by game specialists, is back in residence in many woodland areas where acorns and nuts are abundant. Flocks will range into fields that offer grain, seed, and grass-cover by day, but roost in trees close to water at night.

in playing over a course bordered by woods and fields, and cooled by ponds, streams, or seashore. Here our nerve endings remind us of something essential in not only our own natures, but in all of nature as well: namely, the need for contrast and variety.

In the field of wildlife management, the technical phrase for this phenomenon is *edge effect*. This simple rule of nature says that more life will be found where two different ecosystems meet than at the heart of either one of the systems independent of the other. Hence, more wildlife will be found at the edge of a meadow than out in the middle. And more birds of different species will nest in a hedgerow than in the open field or woods nearby.

To the man with a three-acre, or larger, lot, *edge* is a valuable principle to utilize in planning his backyard habitat. A stand of mature mixed hardwoods will produce seeds and nuts for squirrels and birds. Aging trees contain insects for woodpeckers, creepers, and wrens, and nesting holes for these and many other kinds of wildlife. A field of tall weeds, wild flowers, and herbs will attract rabbits, quail, and pheasants. In some parts of the country, you may even see turkey and grouse. Finally, a large estate will enjoy visits from creatures further up the food chain. A hawk or horned owl may take up residence in the woods, and deer may browse in the field in early morning. When varied environments abut one another to provide maximum edge effect, food and homes for wildlife are multiplied many times over what the area would have produced as one monotonous landscape.

Let Nature Fill the Vacuum

Three years ago a friend who lives a few miles away, and I used the expert advice of our county Soil Conservation agent to have two ponds dug on our respective properties. In his zeal to get his pond looking "natural" as quickly as possible, my friend sent off for turtles, bullfrogs, crayfish, and different kinds of water plants. He spent several hundred dollars above and beyond pond-digging costs on furnishing his little lake with flora and fauna. Working within a more limited budget, I decided to let nature follow her own course of stocking. Today my pond has its share of bullfrogs, cattails, and wildfowl. In addition, I am not plagued by a super-abundance of water weeds like my friend down the road. For in his eagerness to have everything at once, he introduced one plant species too many and now is fighting to save his pond from being swallowed by greenery!

Nature has an amazing capacity to fill voids. The week after the excavation work was done at my place, and while the pond was still only half full, I saw my first water snake undulating across the surface. Wild ducks and herons appeared in increasing numbers, and the following spring I discovered a snapping turtle digging a nest on the sandy dike. Thus the wonder of watching nature populate this new pond at her own pace and with her

The snapping turtle digs down into the pond bank to hibernate. Although generally docile in shallow water where it lives on carrion, invertebrates, and plants, it attacks quickly and savagely if provoked during its ventures onto land—perhaps because its thick, heavy appendages cannot be drawn under its proportionately small shell.

own species has been every bit as rewarding—perhaps more so—than attempting to do the job myself.

Care and Maintenance

A backyard planted for wildlife is a lazy man's dream. You'll have less lawn to worry about than most of your neighbors, and what little you have should be cut less often. It won't be necessary to be out with the pruning shears two or three times a season. Since wildlife likes rambling, drooping branches, I let one pruning per year—if that—suffice. And don't be too zealous about snapping off dead branches and closing up holes in tree trunks. Wildlife has a wonderful capacity for making good use of everything in nature pretty much as it finds it. This gives you more free time to enjoy the creatures who come to your mini-refuge for wildlife.

Since your ideas of what constitutes good wildlife gardening may conflict with your neighbors' ideas about what constitutes clean landscaping, however, talk with them before you get too far along in your plans. Try to intrigue them with what you are attempting to do. Explain why closely trimmed hedges and constantly manicured lawns are unfavorable to wildlife and ask them if they'd like to join you in creating graceful sprawling hedges and casual "American heritage" lawns of native grasses which may even sport a dandelion or two. If you get only pained looks for your efforts, keep your cool. After a few seasons of comparison, the ease, accomplishment, and enjoyment on your side of the fence will speak for themselves—and may yet win for you the tribute of imitation.

The Rights of Wildlife

"Even though a towhee doesn't vote or pay taxes, it is still entitled to life, liberty and the pursuit of its own kind of happiness!"

This statement was made at a public hearing on the future of a town park in my state. Real estate interests and the city council favored building a parking garage on the site. Then a nesting towhee was discovered in one of the park's shrubs, and a new front in the war was opened. Where many citizens had been willing to let the park go in the name of "progress," now they fought to preserve the welfare of a bird. Overwhelmed, the town fathers decided they didn't need the parking garage after all.

A new concept involving the rights of wildlife and the environment has blossomed in the past decade. Christopher D. Stone, a professor of law at the University of Southern California, argues in *Should Trees Have Standing: Towards Legal Rights for Natural Objects* that for the very reason fish, birds, and flowers can't represent themselves in conservation battles, we should be especially sensitive to their rights and make every effort to accommodate their well-being in our snowballing alteration of the national en-

The groundhog is a true winter hibernator. In summer it feeds on field and garden greens. A sometime pest, its burrows are recycled by other mammals, and birds use the entrance mounds for dust baths.

vironment. As people have traditionally used the law to protect their personal rights, Stone insists that we now permit defenders of the environment to enter court on behalf of the creatures of the earth, air, and water. After all, their welfare ultimately means our own.

Some of the same philosophy motivated the National Wildlife Federation to launch the Backyard Wildlife Program (see page 184—Ed.) which is daily recreating more habitat for dispossessed birds and other animals.

The Backyard Wildlife Program

Registering your backyard with the National Wildlife Federation is more than an ego-trip saying, "Hey, my garden is something special." It's a declaration of faith and purpose. It gives you a chance to go on record with friends and neighbors, city officials and businessmen, that you want them to respect the rights of wildlife just as you do.

Excerpts from letters received by the National Wildlife Federation show what a few people can do on behalf of wildlife if sufficiently motivated.

• Mrs. John Wickland has kept a daily log of wildlife observations over the 16 years that she and her husband have been developing their two-acre National Wildlife Federation Backyard Wildlife Habitat No. 25 near Eden Prairie, Minnesota. "I use the records to persuade new residents that they, too, can attract birds right to their windows," she writes. Mrs. Wickland gives newcomers a list of the 47 species of birds which they can expect to enjoy at different seasons, and includes written instructions on where to look for each species and what to feed them.

• Donald and Helen Haugh, a retired biology teacher and his wife, were pictured in their Hagerstown, Maryland, newspaper when the certification of

What more can man desire than to be in harmony with his natural world, to ease away from man-made cares and contemplate perfection in a single leaf?

their Backyard Wildlife Habitat No. 130 was announced by the National Wildlife Federation. In just a few days, Mr. Haugh reported the response: "Phone calls have been many—I give encouragement and information on how to get started. Letters and notes bear the same message. Our pastor is carrying a special notice in the church bulletin. Three Scout groups have asked to visit us. Fellow teachers as far as Frederick, Maryland, have asked to visit. Could go on and on. Personally, this all has been a shot in the arm, too." Since then the Haughs have been in demand among garden clubs in Maryland and Pennsylvania to give their illustrated lecture on how they developed their backyard habitat which has attracted 30 species of birds.

One of the nicest things about the Haughs' letter is that in the middle of recounting their various activities, they pause to comment: "Of all things, a family of groundhogs just crossed our lot, and we've seen several new bird species, including a brown thrasher."

The National Wildlife Federation's Backyard program is power—not power to the people, but power to wildlife. It will add stature to your efforts to recruit neighbors to respect wildlife. Perhaps people in your block can be persuaded to share backyard habitats so that the plantings in one yard will supplement the plantings or pool in another. Your backyard registration can be the first link in a chain of enthusiasm with important results:

• Antonio Spinelli of Northfield, Massachusetts, had to leave his old home when he accepted a new job. But rather than merely sell and move on, he drew up a planting plan for the new owner that was a continuation of work already begun. Mr. Spinelli writes: "The new owner was sufficiently impressed with the natural character of the yard that he has agreed to continue where I left off."

• Emily Kinnaird, owner of National Wildlife Federation Backyard Wildlife Habitat No. 75 in Lexington, Kentucky, wrote to tell the Federation that "The Commonwealth of Kentucky has just announced a feasibility study for the North-South Expressway, which comes dangerously close to our property. Thank goodness we had already applied for this certification! Now, if we can get the entire neighborhood certified, and adjacent neighborhoods joining in, we might 'buy a little time'."

If you own property, enjoy wildlife, and have not incorporated your backyard in the growing network of registered National Wildlife Habitats, then you are shortchanging yourself, your family, and the future of wildlife in America.

A robin's nursery in a crabapple crotch (opposite) plays its vital role in your garden's wildlife drama. As one colorful part of that drama, birdlife answers the pull of the seasons, flowing north for summer's bounty of bug and seed, ebbing south for respite from winter's want and cold. Whether migrant or year-round resident, each species seeks its niche. Thus a duck takes to water, a hawk to a crag, a robin to a lawn where it may yank 10 feet of worms a day.

Robin *(Turdus migratorius)* by Jack Dermid

First Visitors to Your Yard:
The Birds

Northern (Baltimore) Oriole *(Icterus galbula)* by Ron Austing; below, by Laura Riley

by Dan McPeek

The Oriole Slings its Hammock

From an elm in Maine, a willow in Minnesota, an apple tree in Virginia comes a glimpse of orange and a song that sounds like "Eat it, potter, eat it." Thus the Baltimore oriole begins a courtship that may mate him for life. The new parents may return to the same yard year after year—and, with their noisy nestlings, will devour wasps, plant lice, whole encampments of tent caterpillars.

As with many birds, the male's song beckons his mate but also warns rivals that this territory is taken. The victor in a fight between males bows before his lady to dazzle her with a blaze of orange, a flash of black. Colonists named him for the colors of Lord Baltimore, but ornithologists now call the bird "northern oriole."

Later he bullies away intruders as she deftly weaves grasses, hair, string, and yarn into a pouch so sturdy it may cradle broods of mice years after her chicks have flown.

A Home for Hungry Hummers

Broad-tailed Hummingbird *(Selasphorus platycercus)* by Bill Ratcliffe

Ruby-throat (*Archilochus colubris*) by Michael Godfrey

Its nest is so tiny a quarter barely slips in. Its egg is pea-sized; its hatchling is lost in a spoon. But the ruby-throated hummingbird is a mighty mite. Barely three inches long, it may migrate 2,000 miles. Eastern hummers even cross the Gulf of Mexico.

Enormous flight muscles flex its wings at 50 beats a second as the bird hovers, its tubular tongue probing a bloom for a drop of nectar. A man working that hard would sweat 100 pounds an hour. No warm-blooded animal expends more energy for its weight.

Fuel for this dinky dynamo must provide quick energy; it cannot wait for a gulletful of insects to digest, although it does eat some to balance its diet. From bloom to bloom, it refuels every ten minutes or so on the instant energy of sugary nectars. Red flowers attract it best —even plastic flowers on feeders filled with honey water.

Ruby-throat by Dan McPeek

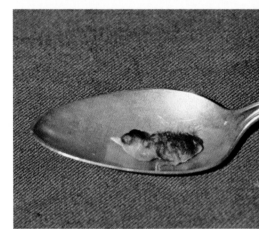

Ruby-throat by O. S. Pettingill, Jr.

Costa's (*Calypte costae*) by Lois Cox

78

Costa's by Bucky Reeves

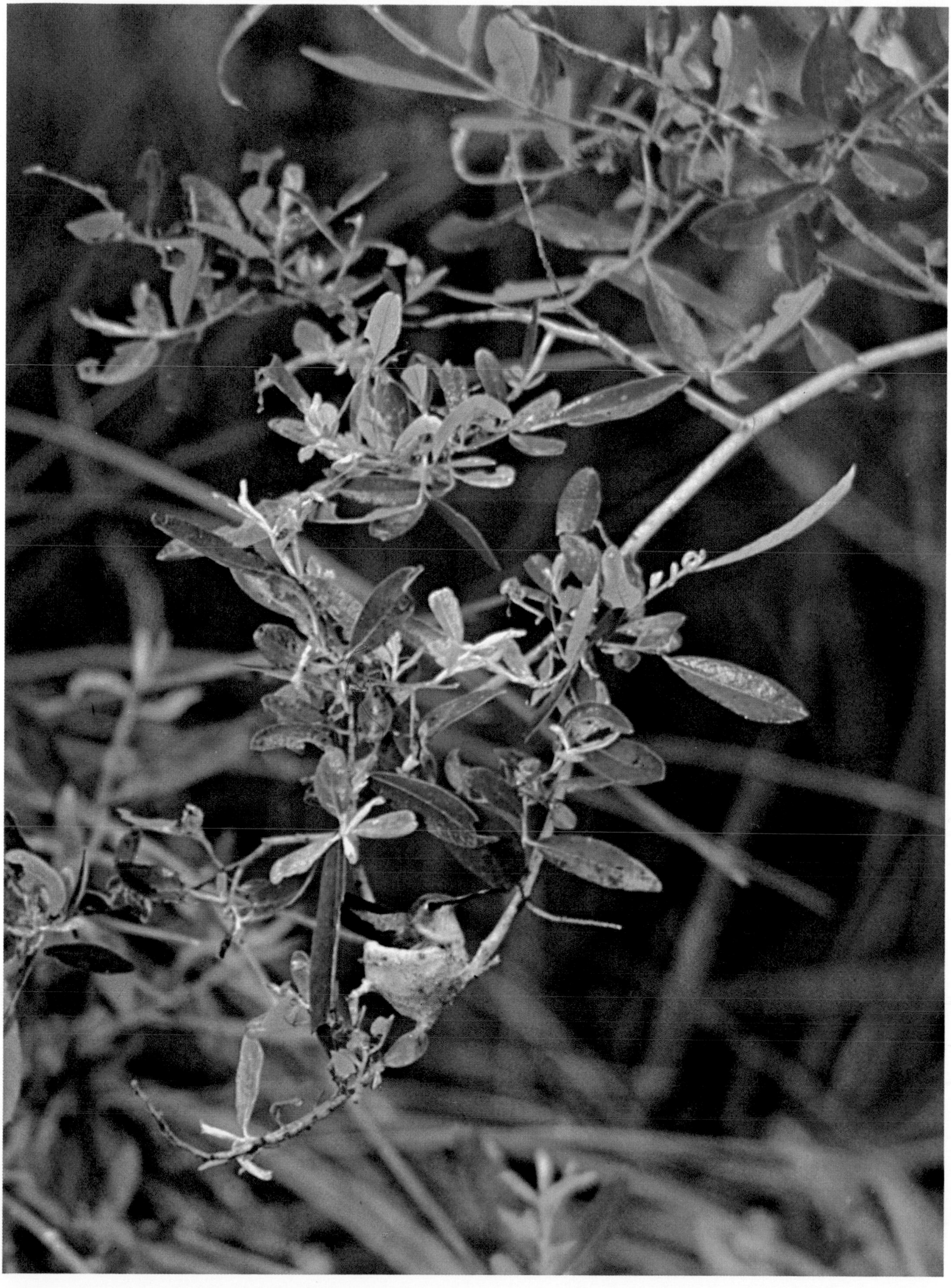

Summer Birds Make a Nest in Every Niche

The bird world musters some of nature's finest architects and some of the strangest. Yet there are no poor nest builders; each ball of fuzz that one day gathers the wind under its wings is proof that the nest it leaves behind was all it really needed.

Indeed, some nests are marvels. The speedy chimney swift, rarely alighting, snaps off twigs with its feet and glues them to a wall with saliva. Flocks seek out empty buildings or swirl over chimneys to plunge in like smoke in reverse.

The whip-poor-will prefers birdland's lowest homesite, nesting on the ground where a hiker may not spot it until it explodes into flight nearly under his boot. The hooded warbler weaves its shallow basket in thicket or sapling crotch, while the bluebird seeks a home in a cavity of an old apple tree. Meanwhile the elusive scarlet tanager roughs out a treetop platform so flimsy the sky shows through.

Whip-poor-will *(Caprimulgus vociferus)*

Scarlet Tanager *(Piranga olivacea)*

Hooded Warbler *(Wilsonia citrina)*

Birds of more than 200 species may return to their nests one day to find their own eggs broken or gone, displaced by a cowbird's larger egg. Some of the victimized parents eject the alien or build a new nest elsewhere. Others lay more eggs and raise the interloper with their own smaller nestlings. Thus the drab cowbird, off-spring of nature's worst —or cleverest?—parents, insures the survival of its kind as the unwanted foster child of the bird world.

Cowbird (*Molothrus ater*)

Chimney Swift (*Chaetura pelagica*) by Richard B. Fischer

Eastern Bluebird (*Sialia sialis*)

Other photos by Hal H. Harrison from Grant Heilman

At a Silent Signal the Seasons Change

Since time beyond memory, man has watched the Canada goose cross the moon and wondered why birds migrate. The key is food. In winter, when southlands fill with birds, there is usually enough to go around. But if all stayed to breed, they and their offspring would overload their environment. Thus birds that fly north to nest, reap summer's bloom of berries and insects there, leaving room at nature's table for the

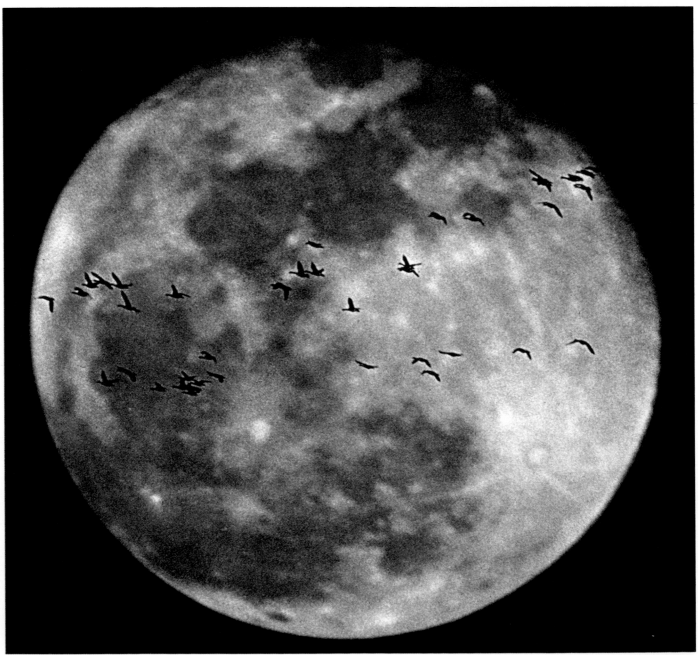

Canada Goose *(Branta canadensis)* by William D. Griffin

summer broods the south must feed.

And so the goose wings to Canada in spring, to Mexico in fall; most Americans see it only in passing. But winter still can feed the millions of birds that never leave. In big trees the shy but striking pileated woodpecker drills for torpid insects and roosts in the hole it chiseled out last spring, while from field or feeder the black-capped chickadee can always garner a seed.

Black-capped Chickadee (*Parus atricapillus*) by Winston Pote

Pileated Woodpecker (*Dryocopus pileatus*) by James H. Carmichael, Jr.

Cedar Waxwing *(Bombycilla cedrorum)* by Ron Austing

Tufted Titmouse *(Parus bicolor)* by William D. Griffin

Blue Jay *(Cyanocitta cristata)* by Walter Dawn

Carolina Chickadee *(Parus carolinensis)* by Thase Daniel

Birds That Flock to Your Winter Feeder

Summer's gone, and so are the migrants. Now the residents take over. Some were hardly noticed in the array of orioles, tanagers, and warblers, but now the tufted titmouse and cedar waxwing stand out in leafless tree or snow. The rowdy blue jay, gentle chickadee, busy nuthatch adapt diets to winter's menu.

All but the waxwing are avid insect-eaters. Bugs are scarce in winter, so diets shift toward fats and protein in other forms. Hang a suet rack and they will visit often. A tray of seeds won't long be overlooked.

The waxwing, like the ethereal mourning dove, loves berries; sometimes it eats so many it can't fly. Raisins and cut-up fruit coax this gourmet to visit.

The brassy blue jay crashes every party (overleaf). But for birds, and for the millions who love them, winter has its own unique rewards.

White-breasted Nuthatch *(Sitta carolinensis)* by Alvin E. Staffan

A Feast of Seeds on Christmas Day

Mourning Dove (*Zenaida macroura*) and Blue Jay (*Cyanocitta cristata*) by Robie Hubley

3|Helping Nature Out

by Len Buckwalter and George H. Harrison

Wildlife will flock to areas of natural cover, concealed nesting places, and bountiful food supply, but the full complement of nature's generosity is rarely found in everyone's backyard. A new home, just constructed on a bulldozed site, may require years to produce substantial signs of a natural setting. Yet it is possible to attract wild visitors to almost any yard, provided there are trees and shrubs somewhere nearby. With an array of feeders, nesting boxes or platforms, and a birdbath or pool, you can enjoy the sight and sound of birds and other animals even while your own plantings are still developing. In fact, there are several ways you can enhance the immediate environment for birds in a matter of hours.

None of these techniques calls for much skill or for more tools than are found in most households. A hammer, a handsaw, straightedge, and—if possible—a drill, are just about all that's needed in the carpentry department. Several items, like screws, nails, and other parts are commonly found in local hardware stores. Your craftsmanship won't be put to much of a test, either, because nearly all the finished products should have a rustic, natural quality. Bright colors, glossy furniture finishes, and precision are definitely out. Sturdiness of construction is the main requirement.

Of course, you can buy feeders and birdhouses—even prefabricated pools. You've probably noticed the growing number and variety of these items in garden centers and even in department stores. But there's a distinct pleasure in building these things yourself, and you'll save a considerable amount of money. Many items you can make from materials that are probably lying around your home right now.

The ultimate reward is the wildlife you'll attract. With the right kinds of food and protection you may even lure a few of the rarely-seen species to your yard. Migrating birds, seeing activity around your home, will drop down for rest and refreshment. Your guest list will probably expand to include small mammals and amphibians as well. This much is certain: investing your own time and handwork can increase the seasonal parade of wild visitors to your yard and your enjoyment of them. And you can start in winter as well as in summer.

The ideal purple martin house has eight to 24 rooms and sits on a pole about 20 feet high in an open area. The overhanging roof sheds rain; the rooms are well-ventilated and cleaned annually in early spring before the new tenants arrive.

The purple martin suffers severe competition from house sparrows and starlings for nest sites. Establishing a high-rise nesting complex will encourage these birds to take up residence in your yard.
Photo by Jerry Imber

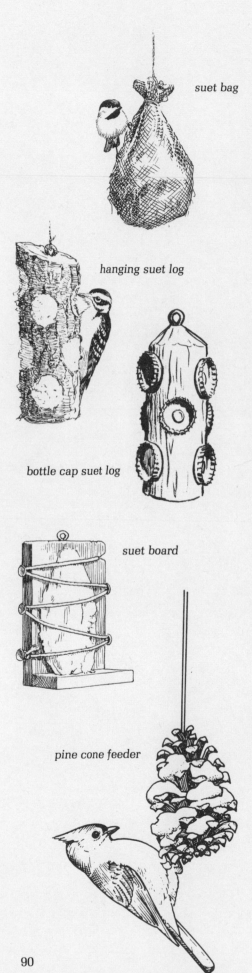

suet bag

hanging suet log

bottle cap suet log

suet board

pine cone feeder

In fact, winter feeding can be crucial to the very survival of songbirds. Natural food is scarce, and cold weather strains their ability to maintain normal body temperature and vigor. It is not surprising then, that on dreary winter days hunger may overcome the natural shyness of many birds and bring their bright, fascinating presence nearer to you—for food now, perhaps to stay and nest close by in spring.

Suet Feeders Anyone Can Make

Of all the winter foods, few can match suet (beef fat) for producing the body heat birds need. One way to catch their eye is simply to hang lumps of suet from a tree or bush. But an entire lump can be snatched away by a single greedy grackle when this important food should be available at all times to even the smallest visitor. Without a method of doling it out over several days, the stock may be quickly depleted.

Consider instead hanging suet in a plastic mesh bag (the kind in which fruit and small vegetables are sold). This makes a fine feeder because it dispenses suet to both small and large birds. A plastic soap dish is also usable, but avoid metal ones because in freezing weather a bird's wing or foot may stick to metal with disastrous results. Simply fill the soap dish with suet and tie it to a tree trunk or limb. Suet can also be lashed to a board or to a tree limb by crisscrossing soft string around both and tying.

A rustic-looking suet feeder is easily fashioned from a short length of log or branch about four inches in diameter. Six to ten holes dug into the wood become effective suet holders. The holes can be drilled with a one-inch drill bit, or they can be whittled out with a knife or gouged out with some other sharp tool. Neatness doesn't count as almost any hole that can be stuffed with a dollop of suet will entice birds. The holes are more functional if they're at least one-half inch deep and cut slightly downward to let gravity do part of the suet-holding job. If you do not add perches, it will encourage such bark-clinging species as the downy woodpecker and the Carolina chickadee, and make it difficult for other birds, notably starlings and sparrows, to raid the feeder.

There are variations on this design. One eliminates the hole-drilling altogether and uses empty bottle caps instead. The caps are nailed to the log, then filled with liquid suet which has been melted over low heat.

The easiest method of hanging a suet log is to drive two nails into the top of the log, at opposite points, and suspend the whole affair with string. Another technique is to twist a small "screw eye" (from the hardware store) into the top of the log and thread the string through it.

To make a suet log for the windowsill or other flat surface, simply split the log lengthwise, smooth the flat side, and make the suet holes. One log will make two feeders.

soap dish suet feeder

Another simple feeder is an ordinary pine cone. Its spreading scales seem designed to trap and retain globs of suet. If cones aren't common to your area, they may be available at a local florist or hobby crafts shop. Cones can also be repeatedly dipped in melted suet to pick up several coatings. Rolling the filled cone in millet or other small seeds right after the last addition of hot suet offers birds a double treat. Pine cones can also be packed with a peanut butter mixture. In fact, most of the suet feeders can take a mixture of peanut butter and melted suet or of equal amounts of peanut butter and cornmeal. Do not use peanut butter alone, however, as it may stick the mandibles of small birds together in cold weather. Pork and mutton fat can be used instead of suet.

Easy Ways to Serve Seeds

One sure way to attract birds to your home any season of the year is to cover a bare patch of ground with seeds. Such an informal method may work for a time, but problems soon arise. Seed strewn on the ground may be washed away or ruined by rain, covered by snow, or scattered by wind. It may also attract squirrels or even rats. Many common household items make fine feeders for seed and other foods. An empty coconut shell is an excellent seed container if you cut away the upper half and hang the bowl-like section from a limb. A wooden salad bowl is also a good receptacle. With either object you may drill holes in the sides for fastening strings. If no drill is handy, place two long strings on a table in the form of an "X". Tie a knot where they cross and you'll have a miniature hammock to cradle the bowl or coconut shell without drilling holes.

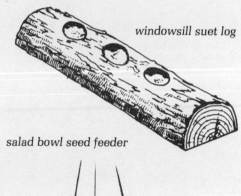

windowsill suet log

salad bowl seed feeder

From these examples, you may be inspired to design your own feeders by recycling natural materials or household castoffs. It can be something as simple as driving a few nails through a board on which to stake ears of corn as a meal for squirrels, pheasants, or quail, or dangling a string of peanuts from a branch for bluejays and other nut-crackers.

Birds Like Variety of Foods

Like humans, birds enjoy varied fare. There are seed-eaters, fruit-lovers, and birds which snap up the concentrated calories in animal fat or greasy doughnuts. Yet, also like humans, birds have food preferences that should be known if you want to lure certain species.

Besides attracting unusual or infrequent guests, selective feeding can also discourage less desirable species. For example, cardinals and chickadees will flock to a hanging or mounted feeder while ground feeding sparrows and starlings will gladly settle for table scraps cast on the ground.

The chart on the next page may prove helpful in attracting birds, but it should be used only as a general guide. There's considerable crossing

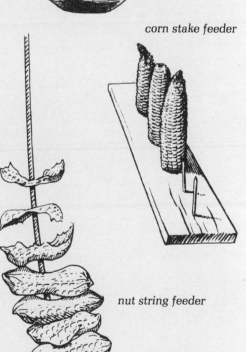

corn stake feeder

nut string feeder

roofed platform feeder

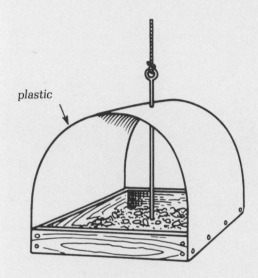

plastic

domed hanging feeder

over among the various food categories, so don't hesitate to do a little experimenting. You'll make surprising discoveries about bird tastes if you present a variety of food at one feeder. The desirable items in a "cafeteria style" display are quickly devoured. The best time to put out food is in the evening since many birds eat at the crack of dawn.

If your trees are still too young to support the small hanging seed and nut feeders described on page 91, or if you want to attract more birds but refill the feeders less often, consider buying or making one of the feed-

Attracting Specific Birds To Your Winter Feeders

BIRDS	FAVORITE FOODS
Blue jay, woodpecker, red- and white-breasted nuthatches, tufted titmouse, chickadee, golden- and ruby-crowned kinglet, starling, grackle, flicker, brown creeper, red-winged blackbird	Suet
Chickadee, purple finch, blue jay, grackle, tufted titmouse, nuthatch, cardinal, goldfinch, grosbeak, crossbill	Sunflower seeds
Purple finch, junco, sparrow, brown thrasher, catbird, blue jay, tufted titmouse, Carolina wren, cardinal, chickadee, other birds when winter severely reduces supply of other food	Doughnuts, greasy crusts and crumbs
Cowbird, grackle, redwing, brown thrasher, hermit thrush, house finch, catbird, snow bunting, horned lark, cardinal, pine siskin, pine grosbeak, goldfinch, purple finch, sparrow, junco	Small mixed seeds (hemp, millet, rape, canary seed, chick feed, cracked corn)
Quail, pheasant, mourning dove, meadowlark, ruffed grouse	Large seeds, (sunflower, wheat, oats, corn, millet, rye, buckwheat, soybean)
Grosbeak, nuthatch, woodpecker, chickadee, bluejay, tufted titmouse, finch, cardinal, catbird, sparrow	Peanut butter, nutmeats
Thrasher, robin, myrtle warbler, hermit thrush, catbird, bluebird, woodpecker, mockingbird, cedar waxwing	Fruit (chopped apple, banana, raisin, other)

removable roof on platform feeder

If feeders are not stocked in summer, nestlings will be fed on plentiful natural foods. The heavier, richer foods above are meant strictly for winter feeding of adults and are not always good for young birds.

ing stations which are mounted on posts and windowsills or suspended from buildings. The three basic styles and some of their design variations are illustrated on these pages. Wood is an excellent all-round material for building these more substantial feeders, preferably boards which are one-half to three-quarters of an inch thick. To slow the weathering process, the completed feeder should be stained or painted a natural wood color.

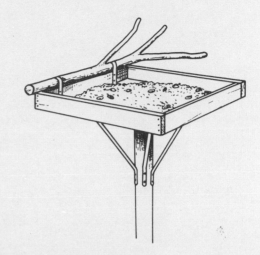

platform feeder with branch perch

The Versatile Platform Feeder

The platform feeder is the most elementary, being a board of whatever dimensions you choose. It may be mounted on a pole or windowsill or be suspended from a tree or a roof overhang. Nailing half-inch thick strips of wood, called lathing, around the edges to form a "fence" one or two inches high will prevent food from being scattered onto the ground.

Adding a protective roof or covering over the platform will lessen rain and snow damage to the food. It's a simple matter of nailing another board on top of four corner posts which have been nailed to the basic platform. Or, if you prefer a peaked roof, nail two boards together at an angle and nail the resulting roof to the corner posts. A third variation of the roofed platform is a domed hanging feeder (see illustration) made by adding a sheet of stiff plastic or lucite and a central-eye bolt to a platform feeder.

The bird-luring capacity of a roofed feeder can be increased by making the top removable. By leaving it off for a few days, the food is visible from all directions and is apt to be discovered sooner. Shy species, especially, are more likely to visit an open feeder. After days of activity around the feeding station, the bolder types will have demonstrated to the other birds that it's perfectly safe. Then, using wood screws, you can add the roof for protection against the elements.

window sill feeder

Adding two or three walls to a roofed feeder will make it even more weatherproof. However, some of the more timid species of birds will not enter if it appears too closed in. To encourage their use of the feeder, consider putting in a glass wall opposite the entrance. You can have glass cut to fit at a local hardware store, and hold it in place with small strips of molding or window putty.

Feeding Through Your Window

Mounting a feeder on a windowsill is simple but you will need to compensate for the downward tilt of the sill by sliding a piece of tapered wood between feeder and sill. A cedar roofing shingle works fine. Use small finishing nails (narrow heads) to secure the whole assembly to the sill.

The trolley feeder is a popular design which will bring shy birds even closer to your window. Moving along a wire or cord, which passes through two small pulleys, the feeder can be halted at varying distances from the

trolley feeder with wire mesh hopper

93

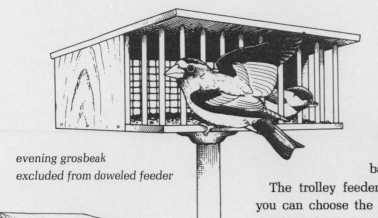

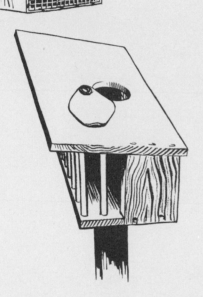

*evening grosbeak
excluded from doweled feeder*

doweled feeder, rear and top views

house while the birds overcome their fear. Attach one pulley to the window frame and the other to a tree or pole. Run the wire through the pulleys and tie the ends to the roof of the feeder. It will then move freely; in bad weather you can bring it to your window for refilling.

The trolley feeder is a great boon to the wildlife photographer since you can choose the distance from which to "shoot". You can also double the fun of watching birds at a window feeder without their seeing you by putting a sheet of one-way mirror acrylic film across the window. It's sold in glass and mirror stores. Because it is solar-controlled, the one-way mirror effect works only when the sun shines.

Giving Small Birds a Chance

Another change in design enables you to determine what size of birds shall have access to your feeder's goodies. It's done by adding vertical bars on all four sides of a roofed feeder, and spacing the bars, or dowels, to exclude the broad-shouldered birds and admit only the smaller species. Dowels are stock items in many hardware stores. If three-eighths inch wooden dowels are spaced about one and a quarter inches apart, only chickadees, nuthatches, and similar-sized birds can get to the seeds. Aggressive jays and grosbeaks will have to lunch elsewhere. The problem can be eased to some extent by stocking another feeder with their favorite foods.

Automatic Feeders For Steady Feeding

A platform feeder can be converted to automatic operation for seed and grain by turning a wooden box upside down on a feeding platform with several small openings cut along the rim of the box where it rests on the tray. The inverted box becomes a hopper which steadily releases a small amount of seed as the food is consumed. The hopper may be filled through an opening at the top. This top hole may be covered by a slightly larger panel of wood or metal held in place by a screw to form a movable flap (as shown in the rear and top views of the doweled feeder).

Two views of a more advanced automatic feeder are shown on the opposite page. Note that the top is actually a door, attached by small cabinet hinges, that opens to reveal two compartments. You can stock coarse seed in one side, and smaller grain in the other side. As shown in the lower cutaway side view, curving pieces of metal nailed to the lower part of the separator panel help the seed flow smoothly toward slotted openings at the bottom. The metal can be aluminum of the type sold for house "flashing," a material which can be cut with tin snips.

Our last major feeder is a mechanical marvel with a mind of its own, the weather vane feeder. It automatically swings with the wind so the opening is always on the sheltered, or lee, side. With a pair of rudder-like vanes protruding from the open side, the feeder turns and aligns itself with the wind. The all-important part needed to make this system work is a swivel under the feeder. The swivel can be made by a pin and socket arrangement: make a hole in the bottom center of the feeder through which you can slide a long bolt (try a three-inch long by three-sixteenths stove bolt). With the head of the bolt on the top of the feeder platform, secure the bolt underneath with a nut and washer. This forms a pin you can insert into a hole you've drilled into the top of a wood post. Keep this mechanism well-oiled. To make the feeder swing, add the rudder-like vanes that extend outward approximately six to 12 inches to catch wind passing below the platform. The additional pleasure, usefulness, and interest which the weather vane feeder adds to your garden is well worth the extra time and effort which you put into its construction.

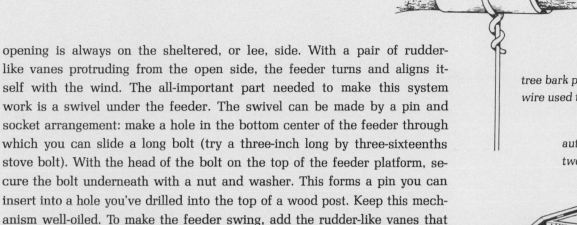

tree bark protected from wire used to hang feeder

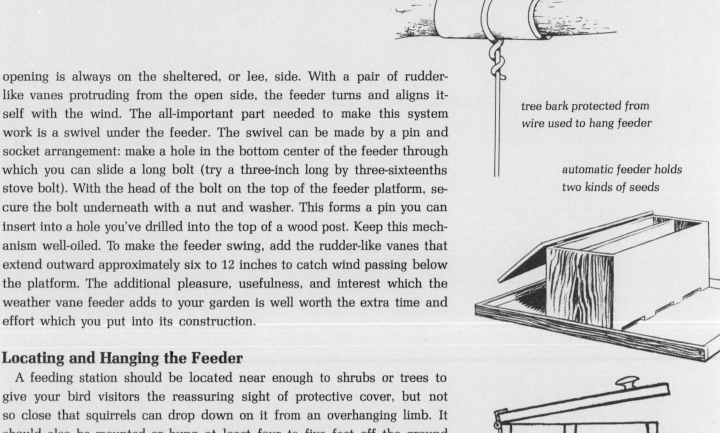

automatic feeder holds two kinds of seeds

Locating and Hanging the Feeder

A feeding station should be located near enough to shrubs or trees to give your bird visitors the reassuring sight of protective cover, but not so close that squirrels can drop down on it from an overhanging limb. It should also be mounted or hung at least four to five feet off the ground with its open side shielded from the prevailing wind. If birds ignore the new feeder, lead them to it by attaching suet to nearby branches.

Be wary of harming a tree's living tissue with wires that can cut through the outer bark. In most instances, soft cord and a lightweight feeder cause no damage, but a heavy, fully stocked feeder is another matter. If you use wire to suspend it, first wrap the bark with a protective sheet of material — canvas, plastic, or rubber — to form a soft layer. Plastic tubing (sold in pet stores) through which the wire is inserted serves as an additional shield. Small nails driven directly into the tree trunk to anchor a stationary feeder usually cause no harm. Nails, wire, and other hardware for outdoor projects, incidentally, last much longer if they are brass or a galvanized type of metal.

curved metal st

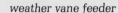
opening

cutaway side view

weather vane feeder

Winter Feeding—A Serious Commitment

A bird's most important activity in winter is finding enough food to stay alive. Attracted by and accustomed to a free and easy food source, birds may suffer if it is abruptly withdrawn before the arrival of spring when their dependency can taper off naturally as insects and plants reappear. So no matter what method you use, understand that when you start feeding in winter, you assume responsibility for the birds' welfare. Your rewards are the satisfaction of sustaining wildlife in time of want and the possibility of seeing a rare species visit your backyard.

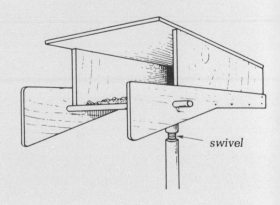

swivel

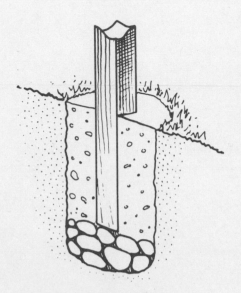

Setting a post in cement to support a birdhouse or feeder means extra work, but it will be much sturdier. The stones at the bottom of the posthole will alleviate the effects of heaving during a thaw.

Birdhouse Design

Although scarcely more than two dozen species of eastern birds use nest boxes, having one ready for occupancy may persuade a winter-feeding guest to stay on in your yard for the spring nesting season. You may even attract one of your favorite species simply by tailoring the entry hole and other dimensions to their exact preferences. In addition, you should make the structure look as rustic as possible and locate the completed birdhouse the proper distance from the ground. Since most birds compete for territory in mating season, spacing is also important. Place birdhouses at least 30 feet apart.

If you purchase wood specifically for the job, cypress is recommended for its durability. Pine works well, too. Sometimes you can obtain wood with the bark still on — called sawmill waste — at a local mill or lumber yard. A birdhouse should not be made of a discarded tin can because the hot summer sun can produce oven-like temperatures inside.

Living conditions inside a birdhouse are made more comfortable with a few simple provisions. If the compartment is not dry and free of parasites, the tenants will be quickly discouraged. Summer temperatures can be reduced by ventilation holes, small narrow slits or holes just under the roof. Since rain or moisture could penetrate these openings, allow water to run out by drilling several holes (one-fourth inch in diameter) through the floor. Cleaning is facilitated by making some part of the structure removable. A hinged roof, sliding panel, or one side fastened with wood screws will allow you to gain access to the inside. By cleaning out the house once a year, the chances of contamination and disease are reduced.

Some birds such as barn swallows and phoebes will nest on ledges or on a simple wooden bracket or shelf-like structure which you can easily make.

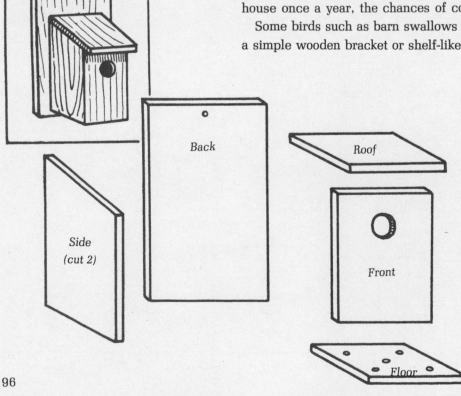

To construct the birdhouse on the left, first cut out the six parts. Whittle or drill an entry hole in the front and five drain holes in the floor. Make the back about two inches higher and wider than the front, and drill a hole at the top for hanging. Pitch the roof so it will shed water by slanting the top of each side panel; the slanting sides will make the roof larger than the floor. Join the pieces together with two-inch nails placed at about two-inch intervals.

Cut a piece of wood four by six inches and mount it about six inches below the eaves of your house or garage. The fastening can be done by two small L-brackets which are sold in any hardware store. Where there is no roof overhang, you can add a back and sloping roof to the structure, as shown in the illustration.

The species which are most often attracted to a nesting box built to meet their particular needs are listed in the chart below. Although the dimensions vary, it is important to use them with precision. For example, the entrance hole must be cut to the correct diameter because it is a major defense against larger intruders. Also, it should be cut the stated number of inches above the floor because birds like privacy while sitting on the nest. As long as these basic dimensions are used, the craftsman can employ his imagination and creative ingenuity to design birdhouses for any setting.

How to Set a Post for Birdhouse or Feeder

The best time to erect the birdhouse is in the fall, giving it time to weather by spring. A wood pole should be treated with a wood preservative before it is put into the ground. For a rust-free metal pole try an aluminum mast which is sold for television antenna installation in both five- and ten-foot lengths. Although you can drive or twist a pole into soft earth, for best results set it in pre-mixed cement which is easily prepared by mixing with water. First put a few inches of pebbles in a hole about two feet deep, and place the wood or metal pole into the hole. Fill it with freshly mixed cement and tamp it down to fill any air spaces. If the pole has a tendency to lean, make temporary supports with two boards pushed diagonally into the earth. Tie the tops of the boards to the pole. Don't move the pole for three days while the cement cures.

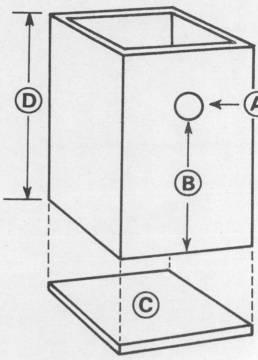

The first step to a custom-built birdhouse is to choose the desired bird from the chart below. Use the corresponding figures for measurements A, B, C, and D in the drawing above. Then follow construction steps detailed on the facing page.

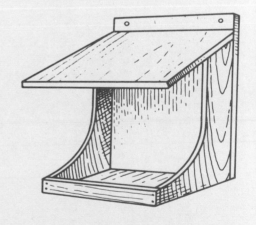

This simple platform will be more likely to attract robins, phoebes, and swallows seeking a nesting site if it is installed in a shady spot.

Dimensions for Tailoring Nest Boxes

| | Entrance | | Dimensions | | Location |
| | A | B | C | D | |
BIRDS USING SINGLE ENTRANCE BOXES	Diameter Inches	Above Floor Inches	Floor Inches	Sides Inches	Height Feet
Barn owl	6	4	10 x 18	15 to 18	12 to 18
Bewick's wren	1 to 1-1/4	1 to 6	4 x 4	6 to 8	6 to 10
Bluebird	1-1/2	6	5 x 5	8	5 to 10
Carolina wren	1-1/2	1 to 6	4 x 4	6 to 8	6 to 10
Chickadees	1-1/8	6 to 8	4 x 4	8 to 10	6 to 15
Crested flycatcher	2	6 to 8	6 x 6	8 to 10	8 to 20
Downy woodpecker	1-1/4	6 to 8•	4 x 4	8 to 10	6 to 20
Flickers	2-1/2	14 to 16	7 x 7	16 to 18	6 to 20
Hairy woodpecker	1-1/8	9 to 12	6 x 6	12 to 15	12 to 20
House wren	7/8	1 to 6	4 x 4	6 to 8	6 to 10
Nuthatches	1-1/4	6 to 8	4 x 4	8 to 10	12 to 20
Redheaded woodpecker	2	9 to 12	6 x 6	12 to 15	12 to 20
Screech owl	3	9 to 12	8 x 8	12 to 15	10 to 20
Sparrow hawk	3	9 to 12	8 x 8	12 to 15	10 to 30
Titmouse	1-1/4	6 to 8	4 x 4	8 to 10	6 to 15
Tree swallow	1-1/2	1 to 5	5 x 5	6	10 to 15

*Nest boxes are very popular with squirrels; often a female will move **her young** from a tree nest to a newly-installed nesting box.*

The sight of a whole family of chipmunks popping out of their burrow and dashing, tails up, across the patio and along private runways in a frantic search for breakfast, is well worth getting up early to enjoy on a summer morning. You won't see much of them in the middle of the day as they nap a lot in their burrow. Unfortunately, to guarantee the safety of chipmunks in your yard it is almost mandatory to forego the pleasure of having a dog or cat, or at least to bell your pets as many families choose to do.

To encourage chipmunks, try your hand at building a stone heap for them to hide in, perhaps to burrow under. Attempt to fit rocks and short pieces of tile together in a way that will keep the pile from collapsing. The result should be a number of inner crevices and crannies. Place plants at entrances and exits for additional cover. Don't expect to have more than one or two families in your yard at a time, however; chipmunks are so much fun to watch because they are territorial and highly vocal in chasing intruders from their turf.

If chipmunks can find acorns, beechnuts, cherry or dogwood seeds, snails, insects, or various green shoots to eat, there should be no need to feed them. But be prepared to see them raid a bird feeder left within their reach or even a low-hanging nest in hatching season. Be prepared, too, for the sight of a toad, lizard, or small snake enjoying the cool protection of the rockpile you built for chipmunks.

Attracting Other Mammals

Squirrels are another backyard favorite, but their lively chatter and undulating movements usually enliven only those neighborhoods in which tall hardwood trees abound. You may persuade squirrels to nest in your yard by building a simple den box and installing it in a mature oak or maple at least 20 feet from the ground.

As shown in the illustration, the nest box, 20 inches high and ten inches wide, is cut from rough lumber about an inch thick, with an entrance hole two and a half inches square. Several drain holes are drilled in the bottom. The entrance side of the box should be attached with wood screws inserted diagonally to allow easy removal for cleaning.

Treat the finished nesting box with a wood preservative for longer life and install it in the crook of a tree, in a snug spot between limb and trunk. Make it easy for the squirrel to enter by placing the hole adjacent to the trunk. Bind the box to the tree with wire threaded through a pair of "screw eyes" twisted into the side of the box next to the trunk. To keep the wire from cutting the bark, you can wrap the trunk and cover the wire as shown on page 95, or you can make kinks in the

recycled Christmas tree becomes wildlife cover

brushpile for rabbits

wire which will gradually straighten out as the tree grows in diameter.

About the best thing you can do for rabbits is to construct a brushpile hideout. One of the simplest consists of leaning discarded Christmas trees against wires stretched across stakes driven into the ground. This forms a miniature lean-to with concealed spaces underneath. Collecting the trees can be a useful winter vacation project for the children. You can also turn a naked young deciduous tree into a bushy winter shelter for both rabbits and birds by tying a used Christmas tree to it. Bind the trunk of the two trees together with cloth strips.

But the last word in brushpiles is constructed over and around a central core of short logs, laid in a rough crisscross fashion to form three or four tiers. Branches, vines, and roots are placed over them, creating and concealing several layers of hiding places. As the bottom logs rot, the upper ones slip down to take their place. A similar permanent brushpile is illustrated on page 134. Ideal for rabbits, it may also shelter and hide a variety of other creatures.

Should We Feed Them?

You can attract small mammals with supplemental winter feeding if you wish, but you'll be responsible for them throughout the cold months, just as for birds. You risk making animals dependent upon your handouts for survival, especially if your area lacks sufficient natural winter food.

Rabbits eat all manner of native greenery from vegetables to the bark of shrubs and young trees. They can also be tempted by rabbit pellets from a pet shop or grain store. They, along with squirrels, also go for corn which you can stake on a board (page 91). You can also make a simple squirrel feeder for ears of corn by shaping chicken wire into a basket, using heavier wire for a rim and cover, and attaching it to a tree trunk.

Neighbors play a vital role in your efforts to attract mammals. To reach your yard, rabbits and chipmunks need travel corridors of shrubs and ground-covering vines, or unmowed grass connecting your yard with that of a neighbor. Raccoons, opossums, and squirrels must be able to travel through adjoining trees if they are to include your spreading maple in their home range. Amphibians, too, must be free to make a safe round trip to stream or pond in the breeding season. Since most of these species also need a larger range than that provided by one backyard they are not likely to take up residence unless the rest of the neighborhood provides for their welfare. So try to be realistic and survey both your yard and your neighborhood to determine how you can help nature attract small mammals there.

corn basket enables
squirrels to eat in safety

stone heap for chipmunks

One habitat element often overlooked is water. Too often it is added last as an artistic finishing touch when it should be supplied first as a life-giving necessity. Yet providing water can be the easiest and least expensive step in meeting wildlife needs. Everyone is familiar with the common birdbath which can range from an upside-down garbage can lid placed on the ground to an elaborate clay or cement dish mounted on a pedestal. Even a dripping outdoor faucet or garden hose can serve as a temporary water source. Another simple but surprisingly little-known set-up for attracting birds is the dripping pail: an ordinary bucket with a nail-hole in the bottom, mounted over a pan or dish, and filled daily with water.

While birds are the easiest animals to attract with water, they are by no means the only ones. The more sophisticated water sources diagramed on the next two pages—the small lily pool and larger waterfall arrangement shown here—will also bring neighborhood mammals in for a drink, and will add amphibians, fish, and other members of the aquatic community to your everyday environment. An artist living on Long Island designed his backyard water hole to be an integral part of his patio. He enjoys a constant parade of songbirds, turtles, frogs, and dragonflies, all moving among the beautiful plants and flowers growing in and around the pool.

Choosing A Pool to Fit Your Yard

While you should envision a pool as the focal beauty spot of your garden, several practical considerations will also enter into your planning and decisions. Probably only those gardeners whose lots are well over one-quarter acre in size will undertake to build a pond large enough for ducks to swim on, and deep enough that fish and plants could spend the winter under the ice, with frogs and turtles hibernating in the mud bottom. Such ponds require the expert guidance which is available from your nearest Soil Conservation Service office. Professional planners can help owners weigh matters of drainage, effects of nearby real estate development, and the safety and liability insurance factors involved, as well as the technicalities of pool fluctuations as they relate to flood storage and the water table. Soil Conservation Service technicians would also be valuable advisors on costs, and whether to line the pond with concrete, as illustrated on the lower half of the next two pages, or with plastic.

Happily, the owners of much smaller backyards can have the beauty of the modest lily pool shown at the top of the next two pages, more than a fair exchange for a few hours of planning and digging followed by a trip to a garden center for plants and fish. Even for a small pool, however, owners will do well to check on liability

A fern-fringed waterfall brings nature's music and refreshment to the garden, and the pool adds another ecosystem to the wildlife habitat. With the gardener's help, aquatic plants and animals arrive, find each other, and keep the water fresh for thirsty wildlife.

A trio of sunken barrels is an easy, inexpensive way to provide water in a small garden. Each lotus plant or hardy lily plant needs three gallons of soil containing some clay (no sand, peat moss, or rotted wood) and enriched with lily fertilizer—one-half pound for a lily, one pound for a lotus. Put soil mixture in bottom of barrel, saturate with water, lay plant root in two inches of soil at a slant, covering all but the growing point. Add an inch of sand; add water until the plant leaves float comfortably.

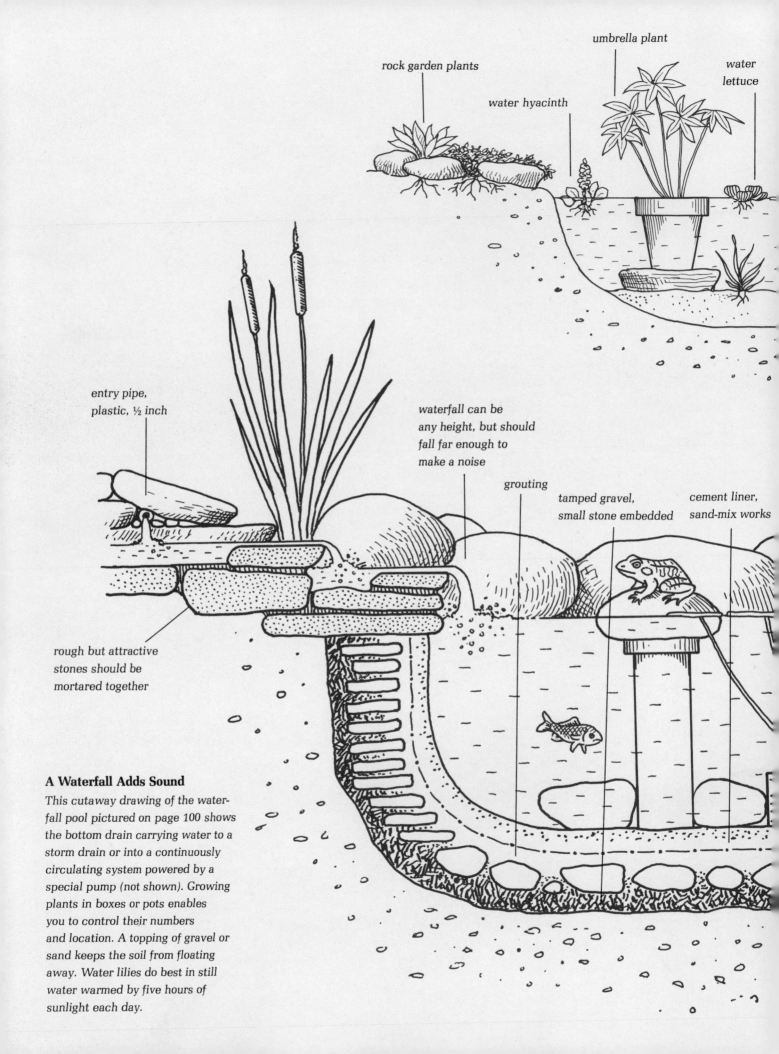

rock garden plants

water hyacinth

umbrella plant

water lettuce

entry pipe,
plastic, ½ inch

waterfall can be
any height, but should
fall far enough to
make a noise

grouting

tamped gravel,
small stone embedded

cement liner,
sand-mix works

rough but attractive
stones should be
mortared together

A Waterfall Adds Sound

This cutaway drawing of the water-
fall pool pictured on page 100 shows
the bottom drain carrying water to a
storm drain or into a continuously
circulating system powered by a
special pump (not shown). Growing
plants in boxes or pots enables
you to control their numbers
and location. A topping of gravel or
sand keeps the soil from floating
away. Water lilies do best in still
water warmed by five hours of
sunlight each day.

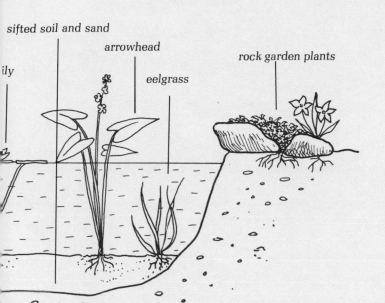

sifted soil and sand

arrowhead

ily

eelgrass

rock garden plants

A Pool for any Yard

This little pool can be lined with
plastic sheeting if soil is too porous
to hold water. Locating it on a slope
utilizes natural drainage which may
be supplemented with a hose as
needed. Properly fertilized, aquatic
plants will grow equally well in
the clay soil bottom or in submerged
pots. Fish will eat mosquitoes but
don't overstock. Allow one inch of
goldfish (not counting tail) for every
20 square inches of water surface.

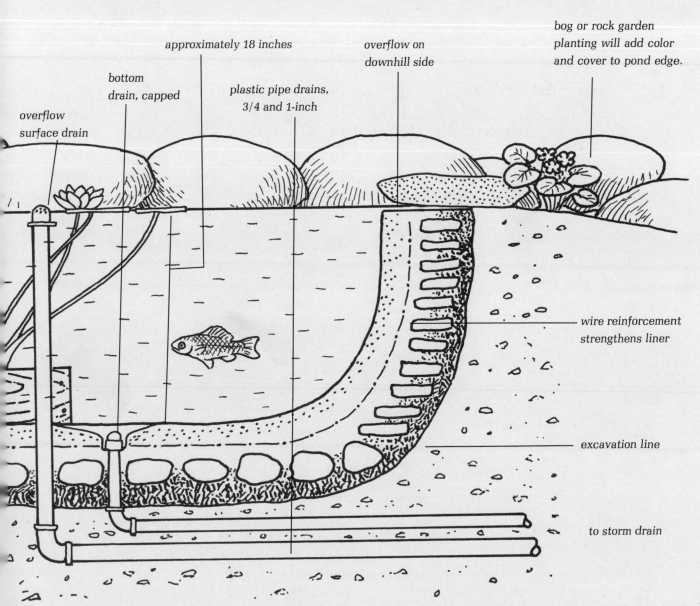

approximately 18 inches

bottom
drain, capped

plastic pipe drains,
3/4 and 1-inch

overflow on
downhill side

bog or rock garden
planting will add color
and cover to pond edge.

overflow
surface drain

wire reinforcement
strengthens liner

excavation line

to storm drain

laws regarding fences and gates for the protection of small children.

A pool 12 to 18 inches deep can support both plants and fish. The soil profile which is exposed in the digging process will reveal whether there is a good clay bed that will hold water at the desired depth. If not, a prefabricated pool made of heavy-duty plastic or of fiberglass can be placed in the hole. Another solution for non-clay soil is to line the excavation with a sheet of heavy-duty polyethylene, polypropylene, or butyl rubber.

Stocking the pool with "good housekeepers"—a well balanced selection of aquatic plants and animals—will keep water fresh and sweet, and limit your own cleaning efforts to removing leaves and other floating debris from the surface. The plants shown in the illustration will aerate the water naturally, assimilating carbon dioxide into their tissues and giving off oxygen. Fish take in the oxygen and give off carbon dioxide. Snails, tadpoles, crayfish, and pond-dwelling turtles do their part by "vacuuming" the pond bottom of plant and animal remains. Limiting plant coverage to about one-third of the water surface is not only esthetically pleasing, but insures sufficient light penetration for other submerged plants.

Goldfish should be added to a new pool after plants have been in place a few weeks. They should be fed packaged fish food every other day (as much as they will eat in five minutes) until the aquatic food chain builds up and the fish can live entirely on insects and their eggs and larvae.

Winter Problems

If your pool is deep enough that plants and animals can spend the winter below the frost line (usually 18 to 24 inches), they will survive, and it is better not to break the ice for them. In shallower pools, however, if electric warmers (see page 130 — Ed.) or oxygenating bubbling devices are not feasible, take plants and fish indoors and drain all water before freezing weather arrives. Otherwise ice can crack birdbaths and even the concrete linings of pools. Birds and mammals can rely on snow and melting ice to keep alive, but they will appreciate your supplying pans of warm water to tide them over the hardest winter days.

Trees turned upside down, a patch of sky spread on the ground, a fringe of ferns and flowers on a rug of velvet moss—to the eye and mind a pond is pure delight. A big pond hosts a wide spectrum of life. Insects and mammals are drawn by its shimmer, or by the burble of a stream or fall. But the smallest pool can mirror a blossom and bathe a bird—and in winter bed down a hibernating frog.

Innisfree Gardens, Millbrook, New York

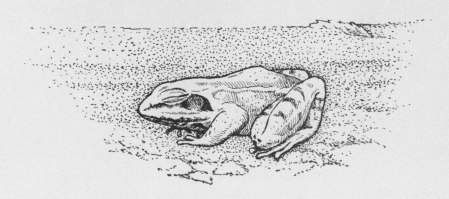

104

The Pond
A Tranquil Mirror
for Your Garden

Through the Looking Glass to a Busy and Complex Community

Peer into a pond, and you visit another world. There creatures float as men do in space, and plants thrive that would shrivel ashore. Life began in water, yet the highest of mammals looks into the pond and feels little kinship with its residents. How great a gulf separates us from the water strider skating on the surface, grabbing insects with its forelegs. Waxy hairs on his feet let this "wherryman" tread lightly on the surface film. He cannot enter the water, yet cannot live long away from it; if his world dries up, some winged forms of his family fly off to wetter pastures.

Goldfish Pool, by Jerry Imber

Green Frog (*Rana clamitans*) and European Cabbage Moth (*Pieris rapae*) by Runk/Schoenberger from Grant Heilman

How different we are from the frog, a cold-blooded insect-eater born of an abandoned egg. Yet how similar; the gill-breathing tadpole soon grows lungs and matures into a frog enough like ourselves that students dissect it to learn of man.

For all its differences, this liquid microcosm, the pond, has much in common with our world. Its myriad life cycles and food chains intersect in complex conversions of energy. And as on land, the food chains all begin with the plants, those ever-spreading factories of energy where the hunted hide and the grazers feed until fed upon.

Water Strider *(Gerris sp.)* by Leonard G. Maynard

At the Aquatic Salad Bar a Free Lunch for Everyone

Large or microscopic, aquatic plants build themselves of sunlight and carbon dioxide and the nutrients on the littered pond bottom, and they keep the hungry fed. The inch-long fairy shrimp gorges on algae, darting about on its back as it scoops up the one-celled plants with waving feet that also serve as oars and gills.

By the time the painted turtle wakes from winter sleep, the shrimp may be dead, its eggs and body settled to the bottom. There the tiny corpse nourishes the water lily's roots. The fragant lily, in turn, hosts an incredible roster of tenants on and under its pads, among its explosion of petals, even inside its rubbery stems. And as the turtle gulps the hapless bug on the pad, it nips a notch out of the green— a little salad with the main course, served any summer day in the pond.

White Water Lily *(Nymphaea odorata)* by Larry West
Fairy Shrimp *(Eubranchipus bundyi)* by Larry West

Painted Turtle (*Chrysemys picta*) by Dr. E. R. Degginger

Green Frog (*Rana clamitans*) by Runk/Schoenberger from Grant Heilman

Eat Until You're Eaten— The Law of the Pond

Fattened on shrimp that fed on algae, an unwary minnow falls prey to the fisher spider, heavyweight of surface navigators. When it's the spider's turn to flee in a crash dive, the hairs that keep it afloat pull down an air supply to prolong its underwater stay. The spider's pursuer may be the voracious frog whose springtime appetite imperils anything that moves—fly, spider, even fellow frog. To the garter snake the frog is dinner, gulped down a stretch throat past jaws that unhinge to receive it.

The pond's law is not unbreakable. Often a creature eludes its foes for a full life span and then sinks to the bottom in death. Scavengers gather for the wake, and what they leave goes to the plants. But if man tinkers with the delicate balance and too many die, decomposing forms may rob the pond of oxygen and choke out all that lives.

Leopard Frog (*Rana pipiens*) and Garter Snake (*Thamnophis sp.*) by Norman R. Lightfoot

Enter the Dragonfly–
Beauty and Death on the Wing

Widow Dragonfly *(Libellula luctuosa)* by H. N. Darrow/Bruce Coleman Inc.

Cat-proof Birdbath by PHOTRI/B. Leatherman

Vital to the pond is the air above it. The lily blooms in air because there the bee makes her busy rounds. For a droplet of nectar she repays the lily with a dusting of pollen, a golden promise of life to come.

One May day a voracious nymph crawls up a swaying cattail. For a year it has roamed the pond bottom, feasting on mosquito and other larvae, insects, minnows, tadpoles, even its own kind. Now it leaves the water for life, and from its split skin wriggles one of the hottest pilots in nature's air force, the dragonfly. Searching with huge eyes, hovering, darting with dizzying agility, the deadly beauty bores in at 40 miles an hour. Bending its legs to form a lethal snare, the dragonfly captures hapless fly, mosquito, or moth. Even the bee can end her vital rounds in its jaws, a tiny entry in the pond's meticulously balanced books.

For a Drink,
a Meal
or a Splash—
All Kinds Come
to the Pond

Rough Green Snake *(Opheodrys aestivus)* by John H. Gerard

The pond draws nature's varied worlds together; around its shining bowl reptile, bird, and mammal find common ground. In the shallows the rough green snake takes an occasional dip, swimming with fair skill, perhaps snapping up an insect before undulating back toward shore to masquerade as just another stem up in the poolside tangle of vines. On the water hyacinths below, the green heron stilts about, beak poised en garde to skewer a fish or frog with a lightning touche.

Snake, heron, and raccoon, high-rise commuters all, work different shifts at the water's edge. Each night the raccoon backs sedately down from its nest in a hollow tree, hoping for a shore dinner of fresh fish, crayfish on the rocks, frog legs—and the rest of the frog as well. The pond is its fingerbowl; daintily it dips each bite in water that is home to countless life forms and host to many guests from the dry world around.

Raccoon *(Procyon lotor)* by Olive Glasgow

Green Heron *(Butorides virescens)* by Dr. E. R. Degginger

Frog Egg   Tadpole

Born in Water
to Live on Land—
the Pond
as Incubator

Metamorphosed Froglet *(Acris sp.)*; sequence by Jane Burton/Bruce Coleman Inc.

Red Eft Stage of Red-spotted Newt *(Notophthalmus viridescens)* by Jack Dermid

From an orb of jelly comes a tiny tadpole, delight of generations of kids. They watch it shimmy in a jar and marvel at tiny legs budding by a tail that will soon shrink and vanish. These larvae look alike until each becomes a frog or toad. Thus some will leave the pond and spend their lives ashore. Quite a different "pollywog" keeps its tail and leaves as a red eft to rummage for insects on the forest floor. A few years later it is back home, as a greenish newt swimming even under the ice for a meal that, in spring, may include its own larvae.

Thus the amphibians—the Greek means "double life"—reenact an ancient drama; their kind were probably the first vertebrates to quit the water and live on land hundreds of millions of years ago. Toad, frog, newt, or duck (overleaf), a tranquil pond enriches the lives of us all.

117

The Pond Built by Man—
a Haven for Wildlife

Domestic Muscovy Duck and Ducklings *(Cairina moschata)* by L. & M. Milne

4| As the Seasons Change

I f you're eager to get going on a wildlife refuge of your own, you can
start today. No matter what the season or what state your yard is in,
there's always something to do, see, or enjoy. To help you fall into
step with nature in your own backyard, my wife and I have put together a
year-round timetable of events, reminders, and tips we have found useful in
20 years of gardening with wildlife in Pennsylvania.

The timetable is only a guide, of course. Nature doesn't work on a precise schedule. Spring may be early or late, fall may be late or early—like
casual guests with a fine disregard for the amenities.

Despite these uncertainties, we've grouped our suggestions by months,
starting off with spring, the time of year when most of us find our interest
in wildlife, in all of nature, at its highest point.

SPRING/March

Often called "the awakening month," March is the time when nature rouses
from its winter sleep. In some northern areas March can still be cold and
dreary, but even there winter is on the wane. No matter where you live,
March urges you to come on outdoors and start looking for signs of spring
—to rejoice over the first crocus, to spot your first robin.

As soon as the ground is dry enough, it's time to do a general cleanup
around the yard and garden. Gather up dead leaves and debris left by winter
storms. Take care of any necessary pruning, but make sure you don't prune
spring-flowering shrubs until just after they have bloomed.

If the ground isn't frozen or too wet, take a sample for a soil test so you'll
know what kind of plant food to use when you start fertilizing in a few
weeks. While you can send the sample to your county agricultural agent
for analysis, you can also buy a kit that enables you to do the testing yourself.

By Donald O. Cunnion

*A robin's nest (opposite) is
usually found in coniferous trees
in early spring when their green
needles are the only source of
cover. For their second and third
broods of the season robins are
more likely to choose deciduous trees
which have by then leafed out.*

Photo by Grant Heilman

The results reveal the degree of soil acidity and whether there are shortages of such vital elements as nitrogen, phosphorus, and potassium. Too much acidity can be remedied with lime while other imbalances can be corrected by adjusting the proportions of the other three elements.

To get a representative sample, take one-half pint of soil from ten places in the garden, digging down about six inches, and thoroughly mix together. Use one-half pint of this mixture for the test. If the garden contains sizable areas of sharply contrasting soil conditions, it's wise to run a separate test for each condition, mixing half-pint samples from within each test area. Another refinement is to limit springtime tests to the soil around trees and shrubs and save the grassy areas until fall, the best time to fertilize lawns. Your county agricultural agent will be glad to advise you on the fertilizer formula dictated by the test results.

Take a stroll around the garden for a final check on the exact spots you plan to set out the trees, shrubs, perennials, and flowering annuals you've ordered. You may find the armchair plans drawn up by the fire on cold winter nights can be improved. Perhaps the tree you ordered to shade the sun porch would grow up so close to the house that it could give squirrels easy access to the roof. Or perhaps certain shrubs could be clustered to provide more cover for wildlife.

New birdhouses should be up by now and old ones given a spring house-cleaning. This could mean evicting some small four-footed tenants, but they can find summer quarters elsewhere. Some of the guests at your winter feeding station may soon be house hunting. Another way of inducing birds to lodge in your yard is to put out nest-building materials—string, yarn, strips of cloth, hair, lint from the clothes dryer. These can be hung from a limb in a loose mesh bag or tucked in a piece of chicken wire in a tree crotch.

If you'd like to encourage squirrels to nest in the tall trees in your yard and you (together with your neighbors) have enough mature oaks or nut trees to assure a dependable food supply, now is the time to put up a squirrel nest box. In view of all the home-seeking and home-building activity about to occur in your yard, it's also a good time to put screens over your chimney and behind louvered attic air vents or windows. If you've done this some time ago, it's worth a trip up the ladder just to check to see that everything is still secure. Birds, bats, squirrels—even raccoons—can be very persistent when they discover an inviting nest site. (See Chapter 5—Ed.)

Pick a fairly warm (over 45°F) and windless day to apply dormant oil spray to fruit trees to kill scale insects and the eggs of other insects that wintered over. Follow directions very carefully when diluting the oil with water. Include shrubs only if they also show signs of scale.

In the South you should be able to set out annual and perennial plants now as well as put in seeds.

A white-footed mouse may occupy several nests in a year. Ousted from its winter quarters in a birdhouse, it may move into a vacated burrow or a tree cavity—or find another cozy corner in the garden tool shed.

This is a good time to clean out and refill the birdbath. Remove leaves from the surface of the pool and replace any water that may have evaporated during the winter. Most pools do not need to be completely emptied and cleaned; to do so would destroy the organic life which has been built up, and which naturally keeps the water clean and healthful. If you are filling a new pool and have to use chlorinated "city water", let it stand for at least 24 hours before adding fish and plants so the chlorine gas can escape. Or you might try a de-chlorinizing chemical available commercially at most pet stores. You can plant hardy water lilies from now through May.

It's time to start looking for birds migrating north—robins, cowbirds, mourning doves, sparrow hawks, killdeer. Maybe you'll see a rare bluebird, or, in the country, a red-winged blackbird. Listen for the first bird songs. You may also see a butterfly or two.

Watch for chipmunks to emerge from their winter hideout.

When introducing fish to your pond, make the transition easier for them by gradually adding small amounts of your pond water to theirs.

April

This is probably the busiest month of the gardener's year. It's planting time. If your new shrubs have arrived and you aren't quite ready to plant, stick the bare-rooted ones in a bucket of water. Or you can lay them in a shallow trench at a 45° angle and cover them with mulch or soil. The latter practice is known as "heeling" and will protect the plants for several days.

To plant bare-rooted shrubs or small trees, dig a hole large enough to receive all the roots without crowding. Set the plants an inch deeper than they were in the nursery. You'll be able to see the former soil line on the plant. Mix the soil you dug out of the hole with peat moss, about one-third peat by volume. Pack the mixture around the roots so there are no air pockets. When the hole is two-thirds full, pour in about a bucket of water. After the water drains away, fill the remainder of the hole with the peat-soil mixture. Build a saucer-like area around the plant to hold rain and any water you apply. Sprinkle a handful of fertilizer around each plant and water it into the soil.

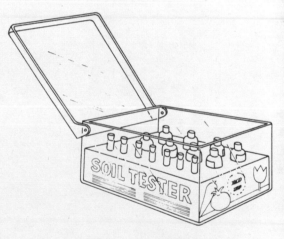

Most soil testing kits are easy to use, quick, and reliable as general indicators of soil content.

Heeled shrubs retain life-sustaining moisture best in a shady, sheltered backyard nook.

Plant potted or balled shrubs in the same way except that the diameter of the hole must be four inches larger than the diameter of the ball of earth around the roots. It's wise to water new plantings every week for the first season. Don't expect too much the first year. By the second or third year they will really take off, the root system having developed adequately. Most shrubs aren't fussy about soil. All they ask is a handful of plant food once a year. The widely used combination of nitrogen, phosphorus, and potassium, sold as 5-10-5, should do un-

less your soil analysis dictates different proportions. Once shrubs are established, many need no fertilizer at all. They just seem to take care of themselves. You'll soon be able to tell which plants need extra feeding and which ones are hardy enough to make it on their own.

Roses require plenty of food. Once established, they should be fed twice annually—about the time new growth starts in the spring and after the first large flowering. We work in some 5-10-5 or 5-10-10 garden fertilizer around the plants, just stirring the soil enough to bury the plant food without disturbing the roots. Healthier roses do a better job of resisting disease and insect pests.

Spring pruning of roses takes place when new growth appears. If you did a good job in the fall, just trim off any dead wood. Cut out weak canes, leaving three or four sturdy, healthy ones per plant. Floribundas can be left about a foot high; hybrid teas, about 18 inches.

Established flowering and fruiting trees can be fertilized now. One way is to put regular garden fertilizer into holes punched into the ground from the trunk to the drip line (the outer edges of the branches.) This is a thorough method, but a lot of work. We just apply fertilizer on the ground around the trees and water it in. It seems to work satisfactorily.

Clean out perennial garden beds, cutting off the dead stems of phlox, lilies, and the like. Clean out weeds and grass clumps, and apply fertilizer. Add new plants to your perennial beds, using plants which should attract some species of wildlife you'd like to encourage. (See Appendix—Ed.)

If you didn't do a thorough job of fertilizing and reseeding the lawn last fall, you may feel the need to make repairs now. Loosen up the bare spots, apply a mixture of seed and lawn fertilizer, and use a light roller or tamp with a board attached to a long handle. Germination of the seed will be speeded—and the birds frustrated—by keeping the spots covered with wet burlap. Remove the burlap as soon as the grass comes up. By the way, don't use lawn fertilizer on your shrubs and trees. Its high nitrogen content will induce leggy growth.

As you get back into a lawn-mowing routine, start now to leave some grass uncut as cover for wildlife. Before you know it, baby rabbits, pheasant chicks, and other ground dwellers will be needing tall grass to hide in. Mice and shrews which enter your yard in their wide-ranging hunt for food will also appreciate your hospitality. Both are themselves essential links in the backyard food chain, enabling hawk and owl, weasel, fox, raccoon, and other predators to survive in the vicinity.

You may see squirrels ignoring your proffered nest box and building a nest in a tall tree now. It will be a large, untidy collection of twigs and leaves. Often a pair of squirrels builds extra nests—one close to the trunk to use as a nursery, others farther out on the limbs for eating or just loafing.

A pheasant chick will "freeze" at its mother's warning call; having little or no scent, it may thus escape bird dog or other foe.

As crocuses, tulips, daffodils, and hyacinths stop blooming, resist the temptation to cut off the tops if you want them to bloom again next year. They are beginning now underground to make next year's flowers and they need the tops to do it. They should be left alone until they turn brown probably in June.

More birds should be arriving from faraway places so keep your binoculars handy whenever you're outside. Don't let gardening chores keep you off the welcoming committee; watch for flickers, purple martins, meadowlarks, swallows, thrashers, and house wrens. Listen for the call of robins, phoebes, song sparrows, and meadowlarks. Nest building should be in full swing for some species. It's well to continue stocking your feeding stations at least through this month just in case of a belated snowstorm. A ready food supply also reduces the time brooding birds must spend off the nest and increases the chances of successful hatching of the eggs.

Marigold leaves have scented oil glands which repel flies, fleas, and other insect pests. The roots also give off a sulphur-containing substance which clears the soil of certain nematodes and fungi.

May

May is the month to do the spring chores you couldn't manage to do in April. The annual flower garden can go in now. Southern gardeners are already weeding theirs. To prepare the bed, work it with a round-pointed shovel or a spading fork, down to about eight inches. If the soil is heavy, add some peat moss. Spread it an inch or two thick on the surface. Add fertilizer and work the whole thing in at one time. Your seed packets will tell you how deep and how thick to plant; also which flowers grow best in sun and which in shade.

Zinnias, marigolds, asters, columbines, cosmos, four-o-clocks, portulaca —all attractive to birds—are easily grown from seed. But for certain other bird favorites—larkspur, snapdragons, and petunias—it pays to buy the started plants. Annuals require little or no care once they become established. Sunflowers will yield a harvest of seed for your winter feeder. Marigolds are special, too. They'll discourage insects and rabbits in your garden, especially the Mexican marigold *(Tagetes minuta)*. The blossom is smaller, but the plant has a stronger scent than other varieties.

Perennials can still be put in now if you didn't do it in April. If your garden bed is prepared, just open a hole with a trowel and insert the plant, firming the soil around it. It is always a good idea to water newly planted material. The root systems need plenty to drink at this point.

If you don't have a birdbath, now is the time to buy one, or even build one. You can find how-to plans in many bird books. Just make sure the bath is shallow enough so the birds won't get into trouble. Without a dependable source of water for drinking and bathing, your wildlife habitat is really not complete.

A forked stick in a submerged, sand-filled coffee can provides a cat-proof drinking perch for birds.

May finds birds still migrating northward. Watch for the indigo bunting, catbird, crested flycatcher, goldfinch, and the northern (Baltimore) oriole. After being around all winter, the junco starts heading for colder climes about now, not to return until fall. Now is the time to keep a sharp eye for hummingbirds. They like trumpet vine, mimosa, and honeysuckle, among other flowers from which to extract nectar. Many bird fanciers attract them with hummingbird feeders, plastic tubes offering one part honey to four parts boiled water.

Watch the birdhouses for signs of occupancy. In open nests you should be able to see eggs and baby birds. From May to August is nest-building time for robins, orioles, yellow warblers, song and chipping sparrows, goldfinches, and cedar waxwings. Keep an eye on the ground for nests, too. If you live close enough to open fields to have ring-necked pheasants, watch for their eggs. We have found them in our rose bed at the very edge of the lawn. The hen broods the clutch of a dozen eggs for 23 days.

Don't be too eager to rescue injured young birds; if you do, be sure they are hurt and not just out taking flying lessons. Most young birds will eat canned dog food, which you feed to them with tweezers. When the mouths open, just stuff in the food. However, wildlife specialists advise that you not try to rehabilitate a bird unless it stands a good chance of a quick recovery and return to a wild existence.

SUMMER/June

June has been called the high tide of nature's year. Every form of wildlife seems to be active. Sit on the bench in your garden, stay quiet, listen, and keep your eyes wide open. As you "hear life murmur and see it glisten," you'll be surprised how much of the nature lore pictured in this book you can discover for yourself.

You may see a toad searching for insects, or a small water snake sunning himself on a stone beside the pool. Those treetop aerialists, the squirrels, leap from limb to limb while the perky little chipmunk skitters in and out of its burrow. You may even catch a glimpse of a box turtle creeping through the pachysandra or something which looks like a mouse hurrying through the grass. If you get a closer look at the latter, you may recognize the shrew with its long, slender snout.

Now is the time when your advance planning for a summer food supply for the birds should begin to pay off. Birds are very fond of mulberries, both red and white, and many types of cultivated berries, several of which are ripe now. An adequate supply of mulberries may help keep the birds out of your private crop of raspberries, strawberries, and blackberries.

By June all the birds that went south for the winter should be back in residence and busily engaged in raising families. There should be much

The song sparrow usually builds an early spring nest in grass and weeds. Summer nests are built up to four feet off the ground in dense shrubs.

activity around the birdhouses. Your maple trees will be popular with squirrels who love the winged seeds.

You can expect some insect control from your resident wildlife. Starlings and flickers eat grubs. Chickadees, wrens, and titmice relish a variety of insects. Northern (Baltimore) orioles consume caterpillars; so do black and white warblers and yellowthroats. Brown thrashers and other ground feeders dine on click beetles and larvae. Hairy woodpeckers control tree borers and moth eggs. Toads eat cutworms. Shrews devour insects and grubs. The praying mantis and lady bug are insect destroyers. So are chameleons. You can buy praying mantis egg cases and lady bugs at some garden stores. You should find chameleons in a pet store.

But the wildlife won't solve all your insect problems. You must take certain measures of your own. There are many kinds of insecticides that are considered safe. The "natural" kind include pyrethrin, rotenone, and ryania, all made from plants. Then there are the so-called "soft" chemicals which kill insect pests on contact, then break down in a few days, leaving no harmful residue. Malathion is one.

Plants, shrubs, and trees are also subject to disease. Both sulphur and Bordeaux mixture (copper sulphate and lime), used according to directions, will safely take care of many of these. If you have disease problems you can't identify, consult your county agricultural agent. But even while you're coping with an immediate problem, be thinking about the basic conditions which may have made your plants vulnerable to attack. The best defense against insects and disease is to put only healthy, disease-resistant seed or plants into healthy soil in the locations where they will get the amounts of sunlight, water, and attention they require.

More shrubs have finished flowering by now and are ready for pruning. Don't let inexperience hold you back. You can get the basic idea from any good gardening book or encyclopedia. If you overdo it, the shrubs will have time to recover before fall. But trim with care those shrubs which bear fruit the birds will want next fall and winter.

Mums should be pinched for the first time. Pinching means snipping off the tips of the plants to delay blooming and to get bigger, stockier upright plants with more blooms. Pinch again in July and once more in August.

As a treat for the birds, let some lettuce and radishes go to seed.

To give the whole family a treat, turn off the porch light these soft June evenings and enjoy the fireflies. Children love to catch them and put them in a ventilated jar just for the fun of observing them up close. If they set the jar out in the yard and watch, other fireflies may gather 'round. The purpose of their light-flashing is to attract members of the opposite sex. Both males and females are equipped to glow and each species has a distinct flash pattern. Be sure to release the glowworms promptly.

Toads are terrestrial, but breed in water; this American toad puffs in a trill that may last 30 seconds to attract a mate.

Mantis egg cases can be purchased but care must be taken to keep them cool; indoor temperatures will cause indoor hatching.

July

If you live in the country and have been thinking about making a pond to hold fish, ducks, and frogs, this could be a good month to get at it. The ground should be well dried out and, if you're building a large pond, the man who operates digging equipment may not be as busy as he was earlier. You, too, have more time now after spring's frantic pace.

A pond with domestic ducks may soon attract wild mallards, which are quick to adjust to the leisurely habit of living off handouts. They often cross-breed with domestic types, bringing forth some of the oddest offspring you've ever seen. Maybe your pond will have room for a domestic goose or two.

Both flower beds and vegetable garden should be burgeoning now. If you haven't gotten tall plants staked against summer storms, do it now. Bind each plant loosely to the stake in two places. If pheasants are getting into the tomatoes or raccoons into the sweet corn, it will also be worth your time and effort to enclose that part of the garden in chicken wire. Don't neglect watering this hot, dry month—shrubs and trees as well as lawn and garden plants need deep soakings at least once each week. If water is scarce, add two inches of mulch after watering trees and shrubs.

It's interesting now to watch young birds getting about. Look especially for hummingbirds. Cedar waxwings and goldfinches are just getting around to building their nests while robins may be assembling materials for their second or third nests of the season. Don't expect too much in the way of bird songs now. This is molting season.

Spicebush fruit should be ripe, attracting cedar waxwings, flickers, and robins well into September. Also coming into the fruiting stage should be red osier dogwood, chokeberries, and various viburnums. Some bird enthusiasts who want to attract northern (Baltimore) orioles and catbirds supplement these fruits by putting out tidbits of apples and bananas.

Butterflies should be around in abundance all this month—and dragonflies darting across your garden pool. With luck you might even see one emerge from the nymph to adult stage and take wing. Look among the reeds or cattails. You may at least find the split skin it left behind.

Young hummingbirds are quick to learn the peculiar art of their rotary flight. They're so small, they are often mistaken for sphinx moths in the half-light of a summer evening.

Wood ducklings usually survive life's first big test, jumping or falling from tree cavity nests often more than 20 feet to the ground or water below.

128

August

More of the flowering shrubs which you set out to provide winter feed for birds should have fruit to offer. These include elderberry, snowberry, and arrowwood. Early ripening apples will prove attractive. So,we've found, will unripe English walnuts.

For several years we thought some kind of boring insects were punching through the soft outer covering of our English walnuts to get at the unripe meat. Just recently we happened to catch the real culprits at work. They were starlings. Next summer we're going to try hanging plastic owls in the tree to scare them off.

Mentioning owls, don't discourage the real thing from hanging around. While owls sometimes eat birds, they usually work harder at eating mice and insects.

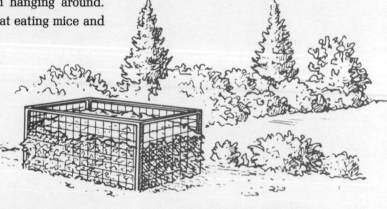

If you don't have a compost pile, the current lull in other gardening chores presents an opportunity to start one— if the weather isn't too hot or humid. The purpose, of course, is to create your own free source of humus, rotted organic matter which makes up nearly one-fifth of the composition of good soil. In a shady protected area erect a chicken wire enclosure which can eventually hold the equivalent of a pile four feet high, four feet wide, and four feet long. One way is to just join the ends of the wire into a cylinder. Start with a base of wire or branches for ventilation, then add a six-inch layer of grass clippings, pulled weeds, and non-greasy food scraps. Cover with a half-inch layer of commercial fertilizer or manure, and two inches of soil. Finally add a half inch of wood ashes or lime and keep repeating this series of layers to a height of four feet. Turn the whole pile once a month and keep it moist. Within nine months the compost becomes humus, and is ready to be worked into your garden soil.

Composting is a clean, safe way to use organic waste; heat in a compost pile can build up to 160°F destroying irksome weed seeds and harmful disease organisms.

This is a good month to try root cuttings. They should be inserted into wet sand or perlite, deep enough to cover leaves or buds on the lower stem. If an outdoor frame is used for bigger cuttings, cover it with clear plastic; indoors or out, it is imperative that the roots be kept moist. Cuttings can usually be transplanted in six to ten weeks.

Bobolinks are heading south now. Orchard orioles started leaving in July. Listen for insect music—cicada by day and katydid by night.

FALL / September

Bittersweet and most other berry-bearing bushes and trees now have ripe fruit. If you know where they grow wild, and have the owner's permission to pick, you may find it thrifty to gather the berries and store them for use in the winter as a supplement to the bird food you may have to buy. Berries should be ripe on barberry, inkberry, winterberry, bayberry, highbush cranberry, and firethorn bushes, and soon will be on hackberry and red cedar trees.

Bird migration southward begins to pick up now for swallows, bluebirds, indigo buntings, kingbirds, northern (Baltimore) orioles, and orchard orioles. Watch for a wedge of wild geese heading southward.

This is a good time to think about putting up new birdhouses for next spring. It gives them time to weather. What about new feeding stations for the winter for both birds and squirrels? You still have time to make or buy them. Do you have a squirrel baffle on the pole supporting the bird feeder? (See page 163—Ed.)

Peonies can be planted or transplanted now. If you have perennials in the wrong places, you can move them at this time with little worry. They will have a chance to become re-established before winter moves in. You can divide lily of the valley and transplant day lilies.

You can also transplant shrubs and hardy plants now, although we stick to the belief that spring is better.

If your garden pool is less than 18 inches deep and you live where winter brings long, hard freezing spells, it's time to take water lilies out until spring. Put them in a plastic bag with some moist sand around the roots and store them in the basement or a cool room. If your goldfish are not hardy, they, too, must be transferred indoors. Remember to use a dip net because your hands could damage the protective slime covering their scaly but delicate skin. Also protect the fish against sudden temperature change by gradually adding small quantities of aquarium water to the container of pool water in which they are transferred.

October

Before it gets too cold to work without gloves, begin the job of protecting plants against the rigors of winter. Evergreen shrubs close to the house can be protected from snowslides off the roof by means of light wood shelters. Damage from drifting snow can be minimized with shelters made of stakes and burlap. Spring-flowering bulbs, tulips, daffodils, hyacinths, and crocuses should be planted now. If you are delayed getting them into the ground, be sure to keep the bulbs in a cool place. This is also the time to dig up, dry, and store the roots or corms of such

An aquarium heater in the birdbath or a warming light bulb in the pedestal requires the use of a a durable, weatherproof electrical extension cord.

tender plants as dahlias, tuberous begonias, and gladioli.

Dead plants of annual flowers and vegetables should be pulled up now. In cutting down the tops of the perennials which have died back for the season, take care not to loosen the roots. If you'll turn over the soil in these beds now, leaving large clods, winter's freezing and thawing actions will make for better soil—including killing the pests which live in it.

Don't burn the leaves you've raked. Put them in the compost pile in the grass and weed layer along with the other materials which you accumulated during the fall cleanup. Many gardeners rake up the dead material in the annual and perennial beds and add it to the compost, but we let most of it lie there until spring so that the birds can benefit from the seeds.

The southward migration of birds continues as they, too, catch autumn's unmistakable signals. If you clean out the birdhouses now, you won't have to do it just before they return next spring, and the spray odor will have all winter to dissipate. To kill lice, fleas, and other bird parasites, use a pyrethrin spray. Of course the cleaned-out houses may be claimed by grateful winter residents as roosts during severe weather. In fact, some people put up separate roosting structures. You can easily build them from plans in many bird books.

Some people start feeding the birds now before they adopt feeding habits which may keep them away from the house. It's a way of insuring the pleasure of their company all winter. On the other hand, putting food out too early may discourage some birds' natural instinct to migrate. You can decide for yourself, but if you start now, you're committed until next spring.

Shielded from crushing snowslides, young evergreens actually benefit from a moderate blanket of snow which insulates them against bitter winds.

November

By now all bird feeding stations should be in operation. Also devices to keep bird waterers from freezing. These warmers can be bought at a pet store or farm supply center. The alternative is to put out warm water every day when freezing conditions prevail.

Fall cleanup work continues. Roses should be cut back only enough to keep them from rocking in the winter winds and exposing the roots. More pruning will come in the spring. In colder areas it's smart to mound the plants with about six inches of soil, then pull it away in the spring. You may want to start pruning certain deciduous shrubs and trees which need shaping or which may become damaged by snow and ice. However, don't prune spring-flowering shrubs now. Their buds already have started to develop for next spring's bloom.

Collect the pruning debris and make a pile in a secluded part of the garden. This brush heap (not to be confused with the compost heap) can be added to throughout the year, and it provides a wonderful refuge for all

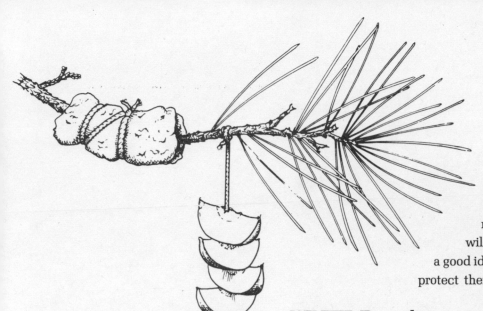

A Christmas tree for birds might be decorated with cut-up dried and fresh fruit, seeds, nut meats, and any summer berries you may have stored. Remember to add grit to suet mixtures—it is essential to digestion, and is often unavailable on winter's frozen ground.

kinds of small wildlife. We add our Christmas tree to the collection. The pile can be removed in early spring if necessary, but you'll attract and keep more wildlife with a permanent brushpile. It's also a good idea to mulch young plants with straw now to protect them against winter freeze and strong winds.

WINTER/December

Unless you are too busy getting ready for the holidays, December is another good month to prune both coniferous and deciduous shrubs and trees. They are dormant in winter and can take the shock of quite severe cutting. On shade trees you'll probably want only to take off low-growing limbs that interfere with lawn mowing and other lawn traffic, or which may be scraping the sides or top of the house. A pruning saw on a long pole does the job. There's also a device called a lopper—sort of a pair of large pruning shears on a pole. You operate it by pulling a rope.

On trees like mimosa and mulberry, corrective pruning is worthwhile. Mimosas tend to branch out near the base when young. If neglected, eventually this will cause the tree to split. Try to establish one trunk at least five or six feet high. Mulberries shoot out branches at downward angles and across other branches. These should be removed for a neater-looking, thrifty tree. For pruning other fruit trees you can get detailed information from your county agricultural agent.

Let ornamental shrubs grow as informally as possible, but by trimming side growth and tops you'll encourage denser foliage which makes them better shelters for wildlife. After the bush matures you can let side growth go and prune the top only enough to keep the bush at a desirable height. Snipping the ends of lateral growth on narrow-leaf evergreens will encourage thicker trees. It's customary to prune holly trees now in order to obtain clusters of berries for holiday decoration. Hollies, too, benefit from lateral-growth trimming.

Now that deciduous trees are bare, it's a good time to look for bird nests which were concealed by foliage. Note the materials used for building the nests. You may be amazed and amused at what you find.

Several people we know decorate a Christmas tree for the birds, tying to an evergreen tree or shrub such foods as suet, fruit, and nuts. One friend with an open feeder on the window ledge fastens an evergreen bough to the feeder in an upright position and ties on food tidbits. Cardinals and blue jays will add their own touch of color to your birds' Christmas tree or feeder. You may also provide holiday meals for juncos, snow buntings, sparrows, mocking birds, mourning doves, woodpeckers, chickadees, titmice, or finches.

You may want to follow the example of other families who have provided a year-round Christmas tree for wildlife by buying a young conifer just before Christmas, using it as their holiday tree indoors, and planting it outside immediately after Christmas. If the roots are well protected by a wrapped ball of earth and are kept moist, and if the tree is not indoors more than a week, it serves the dual purpose just fine.

Still another way to remember wildlife at Christmas is to select gifts which may intrigue others into learning and caring more about nature. A bird feeder, a book or magazine subscription, or a recording of bird songs might do the trick. For the already converted, how about pruning shears or a pair of gardening gloves?

January

With the holiday season over, you'll have more time to spend at the window watching birds at the feeders. If the latter can be located near some evergreens, the birds can enjoy shelter from storms and safety from cats and dogs. We have two Hicksi (upright) yews close to the house which serve this dual purpose very well. Even if you only hang suet cakes or bags on tree limbs, you should at least attract woodpecker types—not to mention the ubiquitous starling. Heavy snows will increase the popularity of your berry-bearing shrubs and trees, especially among birds which do not come to the feeders. We've had them happily eating fruit on the pyracantha, holly, hawthorn, and mountain-ash after a big storm. It is quite a sight to see pheasants sitting in a snow-laden mountain ash feasting on the orange berries.

Most seed and nursery catalogs are sent out in January. If you're not on their lists, watch advertisements in the gardening section of your newspaper and in gardening magazines. Most seed houses offer catalogs free. A few make a charge which is refunded with the first order.

Get several catalogs and start browsing. Take your time learning about and selecting the types of trees, shrubs, and flowers—both perennials and annuals—which will help make your place more attractive to wildlife.

In most nursery catalogs you'll find such wildlife favorites among the fruiting shrubs as bush honeysuckle, firethorn, highbush cranberry, hawthorn, Russian olive, autumn olive, and bittersweet. You'll also find most kinds of shade trees, fruit trees, and many nut trees. However, you may have trouble locating a nursery which sells wild plantings such as silky dogwood, red cedar, sumac, or Virginia creeper. You may have to collect your own out in the fields or woods after the spring thaw. But be sure to get the owner's permission. Otherwise, you will be stealing.

Pheasant, quail, and mourning dove will visit yards bordering on fields and woods. Encouraging such winter essentials as ragweed, bristlegrass, and berry-bearing shrubs is an effortless way to provide winter feed for countless songbirds and for these handsome gamebirds as well.

If you have more time than money, you may be interested in nurseries which offer very young plants at little cost. This material comes bare-rooted and you must carry it along in a nursery bed of your own until large enough to put out where you want it permanently. We've tried these low-cost plants from the Savage Farm Nursery, P.O. Box 125, McMinnville, Tennessee, 37110, and from the Vernon Barnes Nursery, P.O. Box 250, also in McMinnville, with considerable success. We plant them in a special bed, with plenty of peat moss worked in and a mulch of black plastic sheeting. The black plastic warms the soil early, keeps down weeds, and retards moisture evaporation. A year or two in such a bed, and the plants are large enough to set out successfully. You will have provided the labor and the materials which nurserymen must invest to raise shrubs and trees to saleable size.

After you've browsed through the catalogs you'll be well prepared to lay out a comprehensive planting plan for your wildlife sanctuary or to improve an old plan. Then you can place your order for spring delivery, or make notes to take to your local garden center or nurseryman in the spring.

February

If you are planning to build some new birdhouses, February's long evenings provide an ideal opportunity to get at it. Decide what kinds of birds you'd like to have as tenants and then study plans available for each type. Be particular about cutting holes to recommended size.

Gardeners in the South can begin now some of the outdoor work for which we Northerners must wait another month, such as cleaning up the yard and applying dormant oil spray to fruit and nut trees and to any shrubs which may be bothered with scale.

If an unseasonably warm spell should cause spring bulbs to break ground prematurely within the next few weeks, cover them with three inches of mulch or hay. Otherwise they may suffer in the next freeze which is sure to come before their normal appearance 30 to 60 days from now.

Since February is normally a rugged month, be sure to keep your various wildlife feeding stations generously supplied. And don't forget water. Shallow birdbaths should be checked frequently in hard freezing weather.

If mourning doves don't stay around your community all winter, you may now find them joining the other birds at the feeders. Be on the lookout for evening grosbeaks, too. You never know when they will show up, or how long they will stay. A couple of years ago we were visited by about a dozen which stayed around for several days. They crowded the window feeder and we were able to get some excellent color shots. Some experts say not to try to take photos through glass. That depends on how fussy you are. We were happy enough to get the grosbeak shots under any circumstances and took no chances on scaring them away by trying to maneuver outdoors.

A brushpile (opposite) ranks high on the list of important microhabitats you can create for wildlife in your yard. In winter its honeycombed interior provides shelter for many small mammals; low-nesting birds such as the song sparrow seek its snow-laden protection. Even hibernating butterflies may be found here under loose bark or leaf litter. The brushpile's character changes with the seasons as does the character of the community it hosts.

To get the most enjoyment from your wildlife, get a supply of identification books from the library or bookstore and study them these long winter evenings in preparation for the summer.

You'll also want to buy or borrow from your library some books on gardening and landscaping. Among the plethora of good books available, the one we find most useful is Norman Taylor's *Encyclopedia of Gardening* (Houghton Mifflin). It seems to cover just about everything, answer almost every question. Not only does it tell you the characteristics and habits of plants, but also about cultural practices, hardiness, and disease problems. Our copy is thumb-worn from years of use.

Among other sources of reliable information are books by Fred Rockwell and by Cynthia Westcott. You'll find good paperbacks by them and by other writers. Your county agent also has a supply of government leaflets on various planting subjects, some free, some costing a few cents.

A suggestion: in studying gardening publications, don't get up tight about all the do's and don'ts. Many carry a vast amount of detail written for the perfectionist, the gardener who can be satisfied only with prize-winning results. Most of us will settle for much less—and have a lot more fun.

As this calendar of monthly reminders comes to a close, I hope you have found its suggestions useful and that your own backyard is well on its way to becoming a true refuge for wildlife. If so, it is undoubtedly also becoming more of a haven for you and your family, bringing some of the insight and satisfaction expressed by Mrs. Carole Mebus, a fellow Pennsylvanian who with her husband owns National Wildlife Backyard Habitat No. 125. She wrote to the Federation in July, 1973, "As I look out the kitchen door, I see the young pheasants in the zinnias again and a rabbit munching a shredded wheat biscuit. The 'sweet, sweet, sweet' of the song sparrow drifts in through the window. Whatever the pressures and hassles of everyday life, to me this is the real world.

"Perhaps the problem with most people is that they are too removed from nature. The natural world can be more calming than a tranquilizer and more invigorating than a stimulant. No matter what problems beset us, world conflicts, inflation, or the energy crisis—they pale in importance when I hear the 'ee-o-lay' of the wood thrush in the woods. The wrens dart in and out of their nesting box to the accompaniment of hungry voices, and I feel the world will continue another year."

Home is a hollow for two masked rogues (opposite), lazing in summer sun or snugly curled in fitful winter sleep. Unlike the prudent chipmunk, raccoons neither gather nor store food, facing the cold with only accumulated fat as security.

As darkness falls the pair descends to forage alone or family style. Their ring-tailed progeny may hunt a year with mother before they mate and seek den trees of their own.

Raccoons (*Procyon lotor*) by Leonard LeRue III

Spotting Your Garden's
Four-Footed Foragers

Autumn Frenzy– The Search for Food

Any way is up for the eastern gray squirrel, treetop show-off whose claws cling to bark as its tail signals warnings to intruders or its lower incisors pry open a nut. A squirrel's tail is also its rudder on leaps from branch to branch, its balance along telephone wires, its blanket on icy winter nights in leafy nest or hollowed trunk.

A born tree farmer, the squirrel scrambles for autumn nuts to store against winter's want, but it buries far more than it will ever dig up. Forgotten seeds root and mature into 70-foot giants—which drop more nuts for more generations of squirrels to eat or plant. Thus the squirrel's autumnal zeal blesses all who enjoy the shady backyards it has planted.

Eastern Gray Squirrel *(Sciurus carolinensis)* by John W. Signaigo; above, by Karl H. Maslowski

139

The Hoarder's Reward— A Long Winter's Nap

When ice and snow padlock the squirrel's pantry, wise gardeners put out food lest he nip buds from their trees and shrubs. But no one need feed the merry chipmunk, snugly asleep in the dark, silent earth.

All summer this compulsive harvester gathers seeds, nuts and berries, cramming into elastic cheeks up to six acorns or 93 ragweed seeds. Its bad manners make good sense, as fewer forays mean less exposure to its enemies. In a burrow that may extend 30 feet the loot is stored, some in side chambers, more under the bed of shredded grass.

With a snap of winter's fingers, the miracle of hibernation begins. Naps grow longer, breathing, pulse and body temperature sink toward death's threshold. The sleeping chipmunk rouses only to snack on the food stashed under its mattress. Spring brings new food and new chippies. At five weeks each is ready to leave home, soon to dig its own labyrinthine passage to the happy hoarder's life.

Eastern Chipmunk *(Tamias striatus)* by Leonard Lee Rue III

Eastern Chipmunk by Karl H. Maslowski

Least Chipmunk (*Eutamias minimus*)
© Walt Disney Productions

Western Chipmunk (*Eutamias sp.*) by Harry Engels

Eastern Cottontail *(Sylvilagus floridanus)* by Wilford L. Miller

At Home in the Snow—
Winter's Artful Survivors

The cottontail can sprint at 25 miles an hour, live all its life in a few acres, eat almost any vegetation, survive the harshest winters, elude the craftiest predators, embarrass the sharpest marksmen, and mate when only six months old. Against frightful odds the rabbit does one thing superbly: it survives.

When winter bares the branches and hides the grass, the rabbit turns to bark and tender buds for food. Snow is a welcome blanket over its bed in bramble or hedge.

The rabbit's brown coat is easy to spot but hard for hunters to hit. Lacking the large feet of the snowshoe hare, the cottontail keeps within a short dash of cover or confounds pursuers with such a zigzag trail they often give up—while the quarry sits stock-still a few feet away. Cornered, it may freeze or charge in panic and kick its tormentor into retreat.

For these nocturnal nibblers rabbit-loving gardeners build loose brushpile homes. They do this knowing full well the vegetables they pamper and the weeds they pull are all the same to a hungry cottontail.

Eastern Cottontail photos by Karl H. Maslowski

143

Beyond the Fence—
A Glimpse of
Hungry Visitors

Where our world ends and theirs begins, animals fearful of man or ill-suited to his tailored habitat can still be seen. At the woodland's edge the white-tailed deer find good browsing which deep-shaded forests only grudgingly supply—berry bushes, vines, saplings with buds and twigs in easy reach. In hard winters hungry deer crop vegetation as high as they can reach, leaving a "browse line" that trees need years to repair. If spring is late, deer kill young trees as they gnaw off bark, their last stay against starvation.

Tail up like a danger flag, a fleeing deer can exceed 35 miles an hour, clear an eight-foot fence, leap a

White-tailed Deer *(Odocoileus virginianus)* by Harvey Hansen (far left); Clyde H. Smith; Olive Glasgow

gully 30 feet wide. A whistling snort broadcasts its alarm. Scent glands on its hind legs leave a warning for other deer. But it lacks endurance. Dogs, like the wolf packs of their ancestors, may wear a deer to exhaustion, attack and leave it in a reddening scuff of snow.

Gentle of eye, delicate of limb, the deer seems almost too fragile to stand up to winter, starvation, and carnivore. Yet white-tails alone number several million, possibly more than in colonial times. As man thins their predators and clears the forests, life improves for the deer clan —and for the fortunate family who can see them just beyond the fence.

145

Eastern Cottontail *(Sylvilagus sp.)* by Leonard Lee Rue III

First Stirrings of Spring– New Life, New Food

White-footed Mouse *(Peromyscus leucopus)* by Jack Dermid

Woodchuck *(Marmota monax)* by Leonard Lee Rue III

Animals march to the seasons' drum, timing their mating to bear when spring renews the land's depleted larder. Rabbits bear in a month. A few weeks at the nipple and the first of several litters finds greens aplenty on its first outings. The white-footed mouse, snug in burrow or attic, may mate the year 'round—an alarming prospect save for cat, hawk, owl, and its many other predators.

The amazing woodchuck must wait till spring to breed. From about October to March it is locked in profound hibernation. Sealed deep in its burrow by an earthen plug, it cools nearly to freezing, coasts on four to five heartbeats and one breath a minute. A warm snap may rouse it briefly —enshrining it in folklore as late winter's weatherman. When spring's alarm clock sounds, the 'chuck awakes. Pulse, temperature, and breathing rate soar far above normal for at least half an hour. Then out it comes to breed and to fatten for fall.

How to Hunt and Be Hunted– Tricks of the Trade

Opossum (*Didelphis virginiana*) by Jack Dermid

Clockwise from top: by Gene C. Frazier; Allan Roberts; Ron Klataske

With wings to whisk them from an enemy's grasp, birds can afford to be seen; they rule the day. Mammals must run or fight, and so they hunt by night. Raccoons (overleaf) may learn from experience that too many of them spoil the fishing, while the more primitive opossum relies on instinct—whether for a free meal on mother or for a free ride.

The opossum's handlike feet and prehensile tail will get it up a tree in a trice, and its sharp teeth may not have to be used if bared with bravado. If all else fails, the 'possum plays 'possum—actually suffering physiological shock, but looking as if dead and thus unfit for predators who disdain carrion. Its own tastes are far less choosy; it eats nearly anything.

Such a lifestyle must work well, for this prehistoric marsupial—born weighing 1/270 of an ounce and raised three months in mother's pouch—dodged the feet of the dinosaurs a hundred million years ago.

149

By the Pool–A Fishing Lesson

Raccoon *(Procyon lotor)* by Harry Rogers

5 | Raccoons on the Roof

By Jack Ward Thomas and
Richard M. DeGraaf

The old-timer's yard was loaded with no less than 21 bird feeders of all sizes and shapes. We noticed that the trees and shrubs around his house had been precisely planned and planted to meet the needs of wildlife. There were nest sites in tall pines, a den tree among the maples, a berry-laden hedge, and ground-level hiding places in vines and tall grass. As wildlife biologists in the nearby town of Amherst, Massachusetts, specializing in research on the habitat requirements of songbirds and small mammals in suburban environments, we had heard of his success in creating a nearly ideal setup on his modest homesite. We were delighted to be invited in for coffee.

With him we shared a common passion for wildlife. He was pleased and slightly amused by our "discovery" of a scientific discipline which was nothing more or less than the way of life he had been pursuing since long before we were born. And we found on his property ample proof of our favorite theorem—that wildlife exists in any area in direct proportion to the quality of that environment for man.

In advising us on this chapter he said: "Fellows, make sure you make clear that it ain't all sweetness and light. There is trouble to it, there is irritation, and no little amount of heartbreak. When you tell the story, don't forget the 'coons in the garbage can—it wouldn't be the whole truth otherwise."

Raccoons! Who could forget the night when the crash of a garbage can roused the house from sleep? Then the continued rattle of the can indicating mischief afoot. Off with the covers, down the dark stairs with a flashlight, (all the while wondering what bear, skunk, or spirit might be to blame), coincidentally recalling the old Scottish litany:

> "From ghoulies and ghosties and long-leggity beasties.
> And things that go bump in the night,
> Good Lord, deliver us!"

Then the cautious easing open of the back door, the shock of cold night air, the reluctant step out onto the stoop, and, finally, the aiming of the flashlight at—the masked intruders! Up from their work of picking through

The raccoon in autumn begins a restless search for a winter den which will protect him from chilling winds and low temperatures. This bandito has been distracted from his quest by the inviting warmth of the chimney stones. Well-sealed dormers and louvers, and battened-down garbage can lids will insure that he remains a charming and welcome guest.

Photo by Edmund H. Thorne

the scattered garbage for tasty tidbits peer the beguiling faces of a pair of raccoons.

The old-timer's right; an honest book on gardening with wildlife would have to admit that there are occasional problems. Although the problems are relatively rare and generally minor, as backyard wildlife managers we must strive for tolerance of a reasonable amount of challenge. The rub, of course, comes in deciding what is reasonable and what simply cannot be tolerated.

Driven by a deathless curiosity and a discriminating appetite, the raccoon picks daintily through the booty garnered in another garbage can raid, examining textures with supersensitive forepaws as it selects a midnight snack.

Before we are qualified to make such decisions there is an important philosophical step we must take: the step from thinking of ourselves as users of nature to realizing that we are an integral part of nature. This is an enormous step, yet it is requisite not only to successful wildlife management, but ultimately to man's own survival in the natural world.

Take the problem of skunks. Most of us are prejudiced against them because of the unique threat they pose to our well-being. Anyone who has opened his door to the distressed wailing of the family dog and had him shoot into the house and under the bed trailing essence of polecats prefers not even to recall, much less repeat, the experience. Our instinctive reaction is "to get the varmint" by the quickest, most effective means at our disposal.

Yet the "live together in harmony" approach dictates, first, bathing the dog in tomato juice to free him from the skunk odor, and then a clear-cut recognition that, while your backyard may be able to provide the food, water, cover, and living space which skunks need, this is one wild animal which is simply incompatible with suburbia. If you do have a "woods kitty" in your neighborhood, leave it alone, keep the dog and the children in the house, and hope and pray that it's only visiting. Most likely curiosity brought it to your yard, and once satisfied, this unwelcome visitor should return to whence it came. "Kid glove" treatment is called for here.

While we want wildlife in our yards for the pleasure of observing at close range the beauty and aliveness these creatures add to our surroundings, they bring us a greater gift: knowledge of how they live. In order to solve the occasional problems which arise, we are forced to look more closely at what they eat, how they rear and protect their young, and how they meet numerous other challenges to their existence. As our fund of wildlife information grows, we discover that many problems can be prevented simply by anticipating their needs and by giving them credit for their efforts to carry on a normal life in the habitat which our homes and streets have so drastically altered. When we discover a raccoon on the roof, for example, our first move is not to do him in, but to recall or read up on the raccoon's way of life.

What Would the Raccoon Rather Be Doing?

First of all, a raccoon needs a den, for this is the center of its family life. Nature provides this in the form of old trees—preferably near water—where the raccoon nests in an existing cavity high up in the trunk. If the masked bandit has such a tree as a home, there's a good chance he won't seek lodgings in your rafters. Lacking suitable trees, however, raccoons will make do with a hollow log, an abandoned burrow (they aren't equipped to dig their own), or even a culvert thoughtfully provided by the highway department.

Curious and nosey, the raccoon is famous for getting into everything. Among its favorite foods are fruit, nuts, grain, and insects, and when available, such delicacies as frogs, crayfish, and bird eggs. A whiff of a can of sardines is almost guaranteed to bring them in from blocks around. Natural gluttony coupled with insatiable curiosity results too often in overturned garbage cans and a liberal sprinkling of their contents around the yard. To get their neat-fingered paws on the bounty, they seem able to float through locked doors or windows and into garages!

Even if you have a good garbage can defense system, you may discover their presence by the fact that you have been called upon to share your garden corn with them. So the message is, don't tempt raccoons by sight or scent unless you (and your neighbors) are prepared to cope—with wire netting or other devices. In fact, having completed your review of their needs and what your habitat can provide, you may reluctantly conclude that the best solution is live-trapping to return them to their wild world—where you can still enjoy them. It's just a matter of knowing where and when to look.

Since raccoons are nocturnal animals, you might want to initiate a new family activity, a walk along a wooded stream during the first hours after sunset, with everyone carrying a flashlight. You'll find it much more interesting and rewarding than catching their act in the garbage can—and you would be meeting at your convenience rather than theirs.

Like the raccoon, the rabbit is a fascinating mammal that delights the eye and spirit. Yet, because they are notorious nibblers, rabbits are prob-

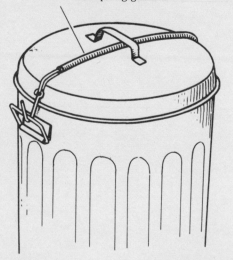

a screen door spring guard

A sturdy box to protect and conceal a garbage can can be constructed with a simple set of plans, a minimum of equipment and material, and a few hours out of your weekend. Remember to include a bottom in your plans for the box; raccoons are clever enough and some strong enough to gain access to the contents by tipping the whole thing over.

155

A squirrel can easily chew through louvers or weakened siding to gain access to the attic or garage, especially when overhanging tree branches put the roof within jumping distance. Covering louvered openings with heavy, half-inch mesh screen will allow for ventilation while keeping out these pert but pesky homesteaders.

When using chicken wire cylinders to protect tender bark on young trees or shrubs, leave space between the wire and the plant to keep the rabbits at a safe distance.

ably not among the animals you'd most like to invite to dinner in your garden. Because they do respond favorably to control measures, however, gardeners have found ways to enjoy their presence and harvest their vegetables, too. The trick is to keep them close, but not too close.

Rabbits need thick brush or brambles for cover and protection, and tall grass or weedy areas for feeding and rearing their young. You can help by letting part of your yard "go", mowing the grass there only once a year—in late summer when the young have left the nest. If your yard borders on a woodlot, don't mow right up to the lawn edge; leave five or ten feet as a "buffer zone." If you will put a brushpile in this tall grass or at the edge of the brambles (making sure it is brush—no lawn clippings, leaves, or compost) you will have ideal cover for many kinds of birds, butterflies, and amphibians, as well as for rabbits.

Grasses and many legumes are the rabbit's favorite summer foods, while buds, twigs, and bark comprise the winter diet. Rabbits may do considerable damage when snow is deep or in extreme winter cold. With no other food available, they will gnaw bark and buds off shrubs and saplings, thus impeding normal spring growth. Some folks actually welcome this pruning job on well-established plants and shrubs, but take steps to protect their younger or prized plantings. The bark of sumac, bramble, birch, maple, apple, poplar, cherry, willow, rose, and spirea all help fill hungry rabbit stomachs in winter. So plantings of these varieties will particularly please your cottontailed residents, and may help to keep them on the positive side of the tolerance-intolerance line.

Fencing is quite effective against rabbit invasions, and probably provides the best permanent protection for both shrubs and garden. The fence should be staked down tightly, or buried in the ground to a depth of six inches. If it's vegetables you're worried about, it helps to leave a good amount of open space directly around the garden plot, beyond the fence itself. Rabbits are less likely to try slipping through or digging under the fence if they must operate in wide open spaces. Of course neither dog nor cat can be expected to share living space peaceably with rabbits. So if you want to see rabbits but keep your pets and protect your plants, you'll need to rig a careful system of fencing the pets here but not there, and the wildlife there but not here. Impossible? Give it a try.

A flicker drumming on the side of your house can be as annoying as it is damaging; it may come as news that this behavior is the bird's way of declaring his territory. And your house's siding provides a lovely deep resonance that makes the drumming that much more impressive! While the flicker will readily accept a nest box, it will probably continue to drum on the house; since you can't effectively redirect these energies, you might as well learn to live with it for the short time it lasts. If the flicker does decide to settle down in your nest box, it will repay you many times by ridding your lawn and garden beds of a variety of insects.

Their World and Ours

Wildlife damage in the garden is one thing, but wildlife damage to the house is something else. The flicker's tattoo on the siding, the patter of squirrels' feet in the attic, stains down the cupola from nesting birds, a burrow dug at the foundation are all small horrors, perhaps, but profoundly disturbing to the homeowner's peace of mind. Your best guarantee for harmonious co-existence with wildlife is to keep your respective living quarters separate. This is a cardinal principle of urban wildlife management, and you'll do well to keep it in mind as you work on your own mini-refuge.

Of course their interest in our hearth is understandable. To a squirrel, finding access to an attic is akin to finding "that big den tree in the sky;" it's a place that provides all he needs in a shelter. It's warm, dry, and safe from predators. For the human host, however, there is the noise, the possible chewing damage to things stored in the attic, sanitary problems, and the risk of fire. In short, squirrels are great, but not in the attic.

As wildlife biologists, we readily concur with the harried homeowner

The yellow-shafted flicker nests naturally in newly-excavated or existing tree cavities, laying eight to ten smooth white eggs each year. Once established in such a nest, the irksome territorial drilling on the siding of your house may stop.

A squirrel in the attic has found the ideal nest site—warm, dry, and safe. In building the nest, however, he is likely to chew up anything you may have stored which might possibly be shredded for use in making a soft nest lining.

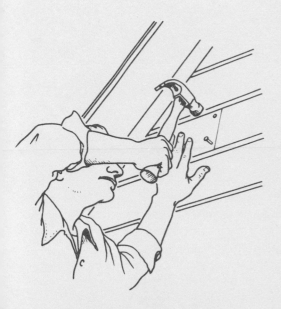

Carpentry work around the exterior of your house to seal up holes, strengthen weak spots, or fill in inviting nooks and niches is a smart preventive measure against backyard wildlife problems. Decorative ledges along eaves or above windows are popular nest sites for some birds; filling these trouble spots with forms designed to fit will make them impossible to use.

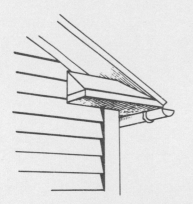

angle deters nest-building

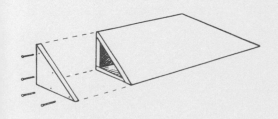

that "that squirrel must go!" But the "going" may be accomplished in a variety of ways depending upon the circumstances and materials at hand. The offending animal can be denied access, trapped, or destroyed. First, look the house over carefully to find out how the squirrel got in. Repairing holes or cracks might solve the problem—provided you make sure the "visitor" has left for the day before you seal the exit. Chewed holes can be covered with sheet metal and painted.

If the critter won't leave the attic, live-trapping is your next best option. It isn't hard on either you or the squirrel. Place peanut butter or other bait in the box-like trap, leaving the door open. When the bait is seized, it triggers a spring, closing the door behind the squirrel and safely confining the animal until you release it elsewhere. Live traps are usually sold at hardware stores, or can be made fairly easily; free plans are available from local U.S. Fish and Wildlife Service offices. County and local agencies also lend or rent such traps. Poisoning or trapping to kill should not be considered in residential areas. If the problem gets too bad, call your state, county, or local animal control agency for help.

Eliminating the nest site is also the answer to the problem of stains on buildings caused by bird excretions. Going after the offending birds is a waste of time, as a new flock will soon replace them. This problem usually occurs in architectural niches where one roof laps another or where a gutter downspout joins the side of the house. To make the particular ledge or hole impossible to use, fill it in with a wooden form carefully cut to fit the space. Birds also seem to like the spaces between the slats of attic louvers for a nest site; often bits of nest material accumulate inside constituting a real fire hazard. Our prescription is to plug, screen, or otherwise repair the louvered opening.

Squirrels, raccoons, opossums, chimney swifts, and bats all seem to regard a chimney as the best possible substitute for the all-but-vanished natural hollow tree they prefer for nesting. The older the house and the

larger the chimney, the more likely this problem is to occur, especially if the owner has not installed flue liners which reduce the amount of space and rough-chinked ledges in the chimney's inviting dark interior. For the homeowner these tenants can generate problems ranging from annoying to downright dangerous. Fireplace draft may be cut off or reduced, nesting animals may create unsanitary conditions and foul odors in the house, and the nest may even start a fire.

If your fireplace begins to smoke and you discover the culprit to be a family of chimney swifts, count yourself lucky if there's only one nest glued to the inner wall. Accounts of enormous flocks of swifts circling around a single chimney at dusk and in no time funneling into it to roost are familair— and true! Swifts also roost in abandoned sheds or barns.

Bats, too, may use an empty shed, the space under heavily-shaded eaves, or just inside louvered openings, but chimneys attract them as well. The brickwork gives them a foothold for roosting upside down. Although traditionally bats have been given a very bad press, these nocturnal flying mammals are actually highly beneficial. They are voracious consumers of various kinds of flies, moths, flying ants, caddisflies, mosquitoes, ground beetles, and bugs. No, bats will not go after your jugular vein, nor do they make any special effort to get tangled up in your hair.

Regardless of appeal or contribution, however, there can be no compromise where fire safety is concerned. A simple, temporary solution to the problem posed by all these uninvited guests is to clear the chimney for winter use by lowering on a rope a burlap bag containing a few bricks. For permanent freedom from wildlife in the chimney, however, install a screen chimney cap. It can be bought at a hardware store, or you could try a little do-it-yourself. Use quarter-inch hardware cloth for the screen, and be sure the cap does not lie flush with the top of the flue so that fallen leaves and other debris would interfere with the draft. Again, make sure all residents are out before you seal off the top.

Chimney swifts once glued their remarkable nests to the inner wall of hollow trees. They have become well adapted to the spread of human habitation now, and use chimneys for nesting sites. Screens to limit their bothersome trespassing can be bought or made, and should be installed whether or not swifts have yet become a problem.

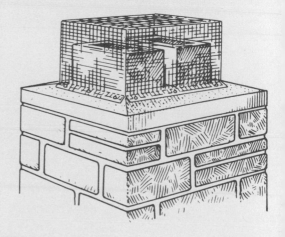

Live-trapping and removing backyard wildlife is sometimes the only answer if your yard has become over-populated or if a particular problem has become too recurrent. The procedure isn't difficult; for example, squirrels habitually travel the same route in their home range. By observing where these trails run and placing the trap along one of them, you can capture these critters easily and efficiently. Once in the trap, they may be released in a remote area where there is an abundance of mature hardwoods.

159

Keep Off the Grass—And the Shrubs and Trees

For those who love a beautifully manicured lawn, there are few things more disturbing than the sight of mole hills and tunnels. There are several ways of solving the problem.

Repellants can be used, but are of doubtful value. Following the directions, you expectantly deposit paradichlorobenzene or naphthalene in the mole's runway only to discover the next day that the mole has relocated its tunnel a short distance away. Poisoning is usually done in one of two ways—gasses or baits. However, results from these methods are undependable, and because of the ever-present dangers to other flora and fauna, poisons in the yard should be avoided whenever possible.

Trapping is easier and more dependable. Various types of traps are available, and all of them take advantage of the animal's meticulous habit of clearing out soil that blocks its tunnels. So it's necessary to know a little about moles' movements. They have two types of passageways: surface tunnels which are used for feeding (and may be used only once), and deeper runways which are used in winter and for rearing the young. To identify a frequently used surface tunnel for trapping, stamp down a short section of several raised runways. Observe daily, re-stamping any re-raised sections until the active runways are known. Stamp down again, set the trap, and the next time the mole comes along to clear out the tunnel—zap! Perhaps the best and most permanent (but most expensive) solution for persistent mole problems is a barrier dug in at the margins of your yard. Use half-inch galvanized hardware cloth, 36 inches wide, and bend four inches at the bottom to right angles to discourage digging under. Leave three to six inches exposed above the soil. Concrete borders or foundations of walls and fences serve the same purpose.

Gardens and fruit trees produce food for our tables, but their yield is equally delectable to birds. Some sharing is probably inevitable, but just how much depends on what else your garden has to offer and how clever you are at keeping them away from your favorite crops.

Devices to scare away unwanted bird guests are as old as agriculture.

Birds quickly become accustomed to scarecrows and other scare techniques. Alternating devices every few days and changing their location in the garden will increase their effectiveness.

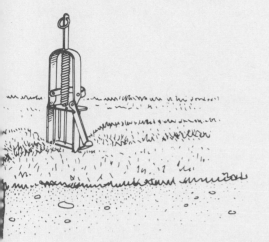

Moles damage lawns and gardens unintentionally; voracious insectivores, they consume Japanese beetle larvae, cutworms, wireworms, and other garden pests in great number. Unfortunately, though, moles kill plants as well by chewing through the roots as they tunnel.

In modern times, scarecrows and similar homemade contrivances have expanded to include flashing lights, smoke bombs, sirens, and contraptions that produce periodic explosions. Simpler devices such as dummy hawks and owls, tin can lids, or aluminum strips suspended to revolve and flash are more suitable for suburbia, though. Scare techniques work only for a while; so try to time them to coincide with the period of greatest danger to the crop, usually when it begins to ripen.

The best protection is to place netting over fruit trees, shrubs, and garden beds during the critical period. Fortunately most suburbanites have few enough fruit trees and small enough gardens to make this a feasible alternative both in terms of cost and labor. Inexpensive tobacco netting, or a commercial netting specifically for bird control, is available from agricultural or garden supply centers. They may not look nice, but it's not usually necessary to keep them in place very long.

When netting some of your larger fruit trees to protect them from marauding birds, you may need another person and a couple of stepladders to get the net in position. It should also be fastened to the trunk or to some of the lower branches to prevent it from blowing off in gusts of wind.

Look on the Good Side

Sometimes wildlife may produce sights or sounds that are offensive in the confines of the backyard or in close proximity to the house. For example, birds sing. That characteristic is one that endears them to most people. Some singing is welcome; a bird song at 50 feet is a pleasure, but the same song at five feet in a sleepy ear may be a pain. Solution? Buy earplugs or learn to love it. People can adjust to conditions just as birds get used to scarecrows. Any species that can live with elevated trains or truck-laden expressways outside his door, can get used to birds singing outside his window. Yet the problem may be minimized. Obviously, you should not plant trees or shrubs outside the bedroom window. Don't allow ivy to climb the chimney and collect roosting sparrows, don't locate the television aerial over your bedroom, don't—well you get the idea.

A Southerner generally counts himself lucky to have a mockingbird in residence in his yard, singing his repertoire through moonlight nights. He grew up with the song and considers it as natural as roses in June. However, mockingbirds have now extended their range into New England and this moonlight sonata may be upsetting to some people who are awakened by

The mockingbird eats quantities of cotton boll weevils and the moths of the cotton bollworm—making its song doubly sweet to Southerners.

it at 3:00 a.m. Its clear, strident song can be heard in the daytime as well as at night. The bird's scientific name, *Mimus polyglottos*, says it all; "many-tongued mimic", it imitates all manner of sounds. Mockingbirds are year-round residents where they occur, and are fruit-eaters. If you enjoy this sweet-singing mimic, it can be attracted quite readily—if you don't mind giving your place a bushy look. The mockingbird likes to nest in thick tangles or in evergreens along fences and streams with fair access to woodsy areas. Small trees and shrubs such as camellia, pyracantha, holly, red cedar, and yew provide ideal nest sites. It also likes the fruit of so many trees and shrubs you're almost sure to have some already: blackberry, cherry, Siberian crabapple, Virginia creeper, currant, dogwood, elder, elaeagnus, grape, hackberry, American honeysuckle, mulberry, persimmon, and privet. Mockers will also come to feeders which provide raisins and other dried fruits, nuts, and suet. Just don't hope to attract them if you like to keep your yard pruned down to a gnat's eyelash.

Overbearing jays and other bold birds often need to be controlled at the feeder. Since they will eat almost anything, the strategy of selective feeding is not very effective, but by spacing dowels close together, as shown, shyer birds can feed in peace. Unrestricted feeders should then be put up elsewhere in the yard for the benefit of the larger birds.

Why Blue Jays Act Like Blue Jays

Blue jays can be irritating at times around the bird feeder; they appear to bully other birds and seem quite gluttonous in their eating habits. The tag of bully, however, reveals man's imposition of human standards of behavior upon wildlife—which doesn't make sense, nor does it reveal an open mind for the study of all the characteristics (both pleasant and unpleasant) displayed by different species. To learn why an animal behaves in a certain manner is to gain insight into the way the natural world works, and also stimulates our curiosity to learn more. The behavior of the blue jay has been developed over thousands of generations and generally insures the survival of the species. Its militant tactics don't eliminate the other common species at the feeder, anyway, so try to keep your mind free from bias about its "undesirable" characteristics—and those of other wildlife species as well.

People also become dismayed, often incensed, at the predator that kills a bird or at the starling that occupies the bird box intended for another species. Again, our advice is to try to adjust your thinking to appreciate nature's ways; if there were no such natural controls, wildlife would suffer miserably from the scourge of overpopulation. The hawk is no more reprehensible than the worm-eating robin, or the seed-eating chickadee. Predators, too, can be appreciated, studied, and welcomed to the suburban scene. They don't destroy their food base, but live off the excess. As with the starling which has appropriated a handy nest box, it isn't acting spitefully or abnormally; each bird is simply doing his own thing.

In any case, enjoy what comes. Study and learn, and fit the bits and pieces together; with understanding comes tolerance and real pleasure. Attempts to referee the animal world will be a frustrating and pleasure-robbing enterprise, and will be defeating the purpose of attracting it to your yard in the first place.

Of course, our plea to appreciate the good with the seemingly not-so-good in terms of wildlife does not preclude encouraging your favorite species. You can always build birdhouses to their exact specifications (see page 96—Ed.); space the houses to take advantage of territorial behavior (remembering that birds of the same species do not nest close together); put out a number of feeders to disperse the activity so that all may feed; and squirrel-proof the feeders to save the feed for the birds.

How To Make A Squirrel Baffle

Protection from squirrels or even cats reaching the feeder from below can be provided with a circular metal baffle or guard placed on the pole four to six feet from the ground. You can buy one or use a discarded garbage can cover with a center hole cut out for the pole, since a two-foot diameter is a suitable size for the baffle. If you make the hole slightly larger than that of the pole and place a collar just under the baffle, it should foil the nimblest intruder; the whole assembly tilts downward wherever it's grabbed. The collar, a pipe clamp or coupling, is a sliding ring which can be tightened in place at any height. It can be purchased at hardware stores. Squirrels are surprisingly good jumpers, so you may find yourself adjusting the height of the baffle.

With more tools and skill you can make a baffle from a piece of galvanized sheet metal. Use a hacksaw to cut a two-foot disk, and cut a slit from the edge to the center. Next draw a circle in the center that is two inches wider than the pole. From the edge of this small circle, cut about a half-dozen slits to the center of the disk. By bending these tabs upward, a hole is formed for the post to enter the disk. The long slit made earlier is to tighten the whole assembly around the post. If the post is made of wood, nails driven through the sheet metal will hold the guard in place; for a metal post, twist some heavy wire around those tabs to fasten the baffle.

When Helping Does Not Help

Upon occasion, well-meaning gardeners may suffer injury or other harm by picking up or touching a wild animal. This is only a possibility, not a probability—and the aim should be to reduce the odds. Our primary goal should be to enjoy wildlife by watching it and *not* by handling the animals. While

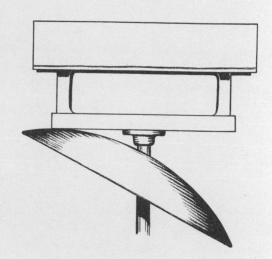

A baffle on the pole of your feeder will keep squirrels away from the bird food and can be bought at hardware stores or made from a circle of galvanized sheet metal. You'll need tin snips, some rivets, and some two-inch nails. Remember that squirrels are phenomenal jumpers, so be sure to position the baffle high enough on the pole; six feet should do it.

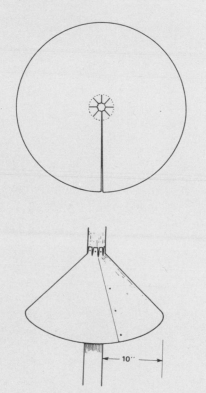

disease transmission possibilities may be remote, they are enhanced by coming into physical contact with the animals, for they do peck, scratch, and bite as a natural reaction to a stress situation. While they can become used to man and quite comfortable in his presence, they are seldom completely tamed, and can become frightened for no apparent reason into biting or scratching. The truth of this statement is borne out many times each year by people who attempt to pet or pick up the "tame" squirrels that solicit peanuts so appealingly in our parks—as well as in our backyards—and end up with a hand embellished with stitches, and a tetanus shot. Anyone who is interested in wildlife *will* probably sooner or later be tempted to care for sick, abandoned, or injured creatures—it's the nature of the beast! Our best advice is *not* to succumb to your good Samaritan instincts.

We have all heard heartwarming stories of animal rescues by persons who seem to have a gift—and unlimited time—for this benevolence. For others, however, failure is too often the end result, along with emotional costs to the amateur doctor. Keep in mind that attention to these unfortunate creatures must be unstinting in most cases; you won't be able to put down dishes of food and water in the morning, leave for school or work, and come home in the evening expecting to follow your usual routine, much less enjoy an occasional evening out. Feeding must often be done by hand, and young animals especially need attention at frequent intervals around the clock. Caring for even healthy domestic animals demands a certain amount of work and a responsible adjustment of your schedule to their needs. Throw in a broken wing or a case of exposure and you have a lot of overtime hours in your future!

What About Rabies?

Inconvenience is not the only price of doctoring wildlife. Contagious disease is also a threat to the non-professional. Although it is unlikely that you will come in contact with a carrier of rabies, your pets must be inoculated at recommended intervals especially if they spend any time outdoors, and absolutely if they run in open countryside. A few species of wild animals do carry this much-feared disease and this fact should not be minimized.

Contrary to popular belief, an animal need not be foaming at the mouth, snapping and growling at nothing, or exhibiting any of the other symptoms to be infected with rabies; some, in fact, may incubate the virus in their bodies for up to a year with none of the usual outward manifestations. Outbreaks occur when wild populations of the carrier species become too dense for the local environment to support them in a healthy state, and it is these animals who infect our pets and thus endanger us. The threat is diminishing as inoculation programs become stronger; incidence of rabies among household pets has decreased markedly, while it is on the increase among wild

A bird nest in the rain gutter (opposite) may delight you, but troublesome clogging, or soiling of roof and siding, will not. You may be tempted to perform occasional rescues of the young birds. Lacking accommodating twigs and branches, test flights can end in abrupt landings. Tougher than you'd guess, the resilient fledgling will probably go on to finish flying lessons on the ground, supervised by its vigilant mother. Such problems can be avoided by fastening screen or hardware cloth over your rain gutters.

Snowmobiles should be operated only in accordance with state and local ordinances, and care taken not to trespass on private property. Aside from the obvious problems in open countryside of chasing and exhausting game, damaging young trees, and creating offensive noise, the unnaturally and irregularly packed snow left in the wake of these vehicles affects the flora and fauna beneath it. Altered temperatures and changes in the melting rate during a thaw are two such problems which will probably have long-term impact on the environment.

animals (foxes, skunks, bats, and raccoons) where favorable habitat conditions exist and protective game laws may create over-crowding, and eventually unhealthy animals. Taking in wildlife waifs is taking a chance.

If you do take orphans or hurt or injured wildlife into your care, first, wear gloves when handling the animal, and second, get it to the vet immediately. Necessary shots, and tests for communicable diseases (such as salmonella in birds) can be done straight away, thus avoiding unnecessary risks. Be prepared to spend a fair amount of money at the veterinarian's and the pet shop for various medicines and dietary supplements.

Finally, laws against keeping wildlife in captivity may be broken in the process of taking in and caring for wild animals. It may sound heartless, but these are some of the reasons why we say most wildlife thought to be lost or abandoned is better left alone.

People Problems

Sad to say, all of the problems which may arise in gardening with wildlife are not caused by animals. A plea frequently addressed to the National Wildlife Federation by its certified Backyard Wildlife Habitat owners is, "Tell us what to do about snowmobiles trespassing on our property, damaging shrubs, and frightening wildlife away from winter feeding stations." While this problem is unique to unfenced backyards which abut a park or open country, the long-term effect of snowmobiles on the total environment is a matter which concerns us all. The maintenance and safeguarding of all natural habitats rely on good will and efforts to keep them in good condition for both man and wildlife.

When problems arise, the snowmobile itself—as with most products of our technological society—is not the offender. Rather it is the few people who misuse such machines and abuse the environment. This constitutes the lasting threat. Remember that as property owners, you are entitled to protect your land by fencing and posting signs indicating that the area is being used as a wildlife haven and is not to be disturbed. Violations of local snowmobile ordinances should be reported.

Most people problems in urban wildlife management are not quite so exotic, and in fact are often found right next door. For instance, boys will sometimes stalk birds with BB guns, killing some and scaring many more away from an area. In the general scheme of things, the boys are acting as predators and are not apt to permanently reduce the wildlife population. Still, after repeated disruptions of this sort, the birds may seek greener, quieter pastures, and all your habitat plans will come to naught, at least for a time.

This problem may be handled in any one of three common-sense ways: a talk with the culprit, a talk with his parents, or, as a last resort, a talk with local police. Dealing directly with the youngster is undoubtedly best—if you can catch him—but talking with his parents can be beneficial in a different way. Aside from settling the pot-shot issue, your explanation of what you are trying to do may interest another family in the backyard wildlife idea. Your own habitat efforts can be aided greatly by the participation of neighbors whose backyards adjoin yours.

Where to Turn for Help

Fortunately, the problems encountered by most backyard wildlife hosts are minor, and professional assistance is usually not far away when it's needed.

Try to convince your neighbors of the value of joining forces to create a more extensive, continuous mini-refuge. Sharing and contributing to a common hedge row, for instance, would increase the area attractive to birds, small mammals, and other forms of wildlife. Agreeing to let the grass grow tall next to the hedge would extend safe travel routes for small mammals. It would also give the neighborhood a uniformly natural look, smoothing the transition from hedge to clipped grass on both sides, and creating a more complete habitat.

Information and counsel are available in varying degrees from private organizations such as the National Wildlife Federation, the Audubon Society, garden clubs, and local nature centers. Also, most major newspapers have garden editors and outdoor columnists who give advice and pass along tips to the wildlife gardening fraternity.

Among government agencies, the best bets for help in attracting and controlling wildlife at the federal level are the U.S. Fish and Wildlife Service and the Soil Conservation Service. Many state wildlife agencies are prepared to help, but usually devote most of their attention to game. A push for proper funding by these agencies could make more assistance available to owners of backyard wildlife habitats and the citizens who strive to create and maintain them.

If fumigation or poisoning becomes imperative, remember this is a job best left to professionals. The yellow pages of the telephone book will give you a list of exterminator firms to choose from. This is one job worth doing well.

One of the most reliable local sources of help in every state is the county agricultural agent. Municipal animal control units are also helpful. Several progressive communities now employ a conservationist to deal with urban wildlife problems. May their tribe increase!

Is It Worth It?

We firmly believe that the returns from an active backyard wildlife habitat program are worth all the costs. Most of all, we believe that the wildlife surrounding a home is an indication of the quality of that environment for man. Visualize a neighborhood resplendent with birds and other animals of all sizes and colors, all the variety of life histories, all the fascinating kinds of behavior. Why are these creatures found here and not across the way? Even a superficial examination will reveal the deciding difference in the types of vegetation, their arrangement, how the yard is kept, and so on. The worries, if any occur, will be minor compared to the enjoyment and the ecological insights derived. All the pleasure in sharing your yard with wildlife builds slowly toward understanding not only wildlife, but man—how we, too, live and fare in relationship to the earth that supplies us with our cover, food, water, and living space.

Are your time and effort and forebearance worth it? You bet!

A furry bandit pilfers a seed—and in the blink of a shutter a young cameraman makes the moment immortal. Who can guess what may happen in the very next minute as wild creatures stage the best show in town and make it up as they go along? Many people are content to look, catching vignettes a glance at a time; others watch carefully, jotting notes, taking pictures, seeking insights, gaining understanding. Either way, investing in time and tools can bring you closer to the myriad living things that share the natural world with you.

Photo by George H. Harrison

The Best Show
In Town

Getting Closer to Nature

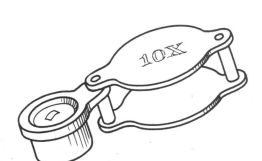

A camera or tape recorder can bring wildlife startlingly close—and so can a simple magnifier, whether on hikes in the wild or strolls in the yard. Opened to the world in the palm of your hand, it turns a seed into a sculpture, a gnat into a dragon, a tiny blossom on a lawn weed into an orchid of exquisite grace and hue.

For a dollar or two, a magnifier takes you into a world of tiny wonders you never saw before. Few investments so small repay the nature lover so well. A camera need not cost much more to yield good wildlife photos in color or black and white.

Even a simple aim-and-shoot can bag a deer for your album—and teach you to keep backgrounds simple, camera steady, subject at ease, and yourself patient and observant. But as you improve, so should your equipment. A better camera lets you slow the shutter to paint a blur of wings at the birdbath, then speed it up to catch every feather talon-sharp. A flashgun helps freeze fast action with its instant burst of light; detached from the

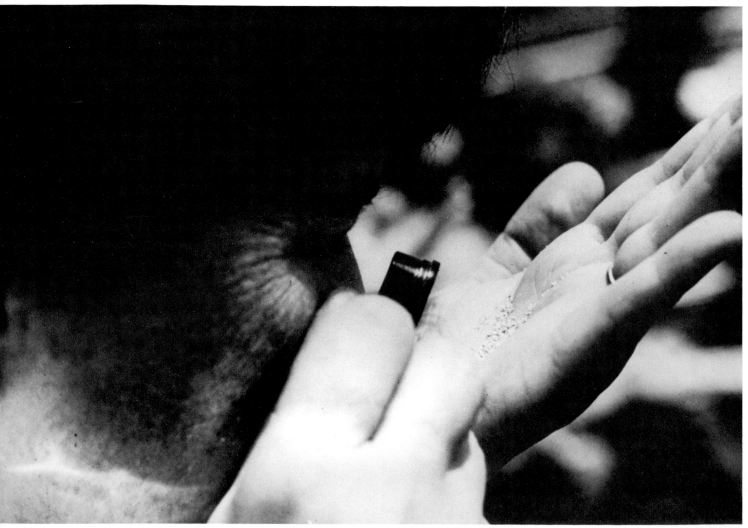

George H. Harrison

Ivan L. Marx

camera it can model the subject in sidelight and keep the background dark. A sturdy tripod holds everything steady while you and a ground squirrel focus on each other, or while birds bathe and you squeeze the shutter with a long cable release. To pull shy visitors close, try a telephoto lens; use it with tripod and fast shutter since it magnifies camera movement too.

A microphone also shrinks distance, bringing bird song or squirrel chatter to your recorder. Hang it where your subjects gather, then tape a living library—or plug it into your hi-fi and just listen as your guests ad-lib about backyard events.

171

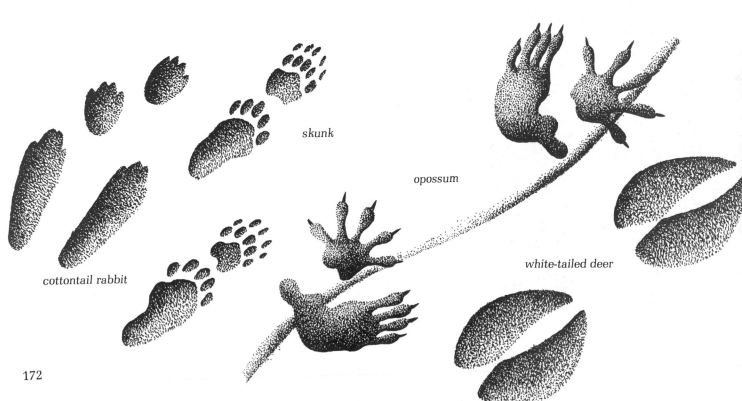

skunk

opossum

cottontail rabbit

white-tailed deer

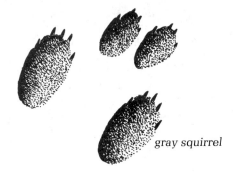
gray squirrel

George H. Harrison

Les Blacklock

Enjoying the Garden in New Ways

You've invited wildlife back, and they've come; now it's their yard as well as yours, and time to get better acquainted. Spend a summer night under the sky and awake to the traffic of birds at your feeder. Keep a flashlight beside your sleeping bag for an owl's view of night visitors. Most will tolerate its glare long enough to make waking worthwhile.

Since all life comes from the soil, let the children tell you what yours contains. From a sample bored by an earth auger or dug with a trowel, they can identify sand, clay, or loam and match up seed packet planting directions accordingly.

Don't let cold weather stop you. In winter snow—as in summer mud— each animal signs nature's register with tracks uniquely its own. Early risers see the best prints, before sun and wind disturb the outlines. Look them up in a good field guide; learn to "read" an unhurried walk, a frantic dash for cover, and the drama of predator and prey where two paths meet and only one continues on.

Discovering What's New in the Backyard

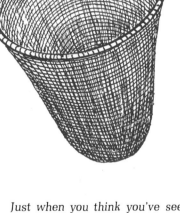

Just when you think you've seen it all, a new star bows onstage. Perhaps that young garter snake was there all along, snatching insects and dodging predators that make a snake a snack. But it took inquisitive eyes and a little luck to spot it sunning on a rock. And it took a fast hand to catch it before it fled.

When more than a hand is needed, a long-handled net works wonders. It can seine the pond for frogs, tadpoles, turtles. It can sift the breeze for butterflies, fireflies, craneflies, houseflies. Even a small one can pull from the shallows enough oddities to make a young naturalist's jaw drop.

In the right hands, equipment need not be elaborate. A bit of mesh on a pole—and a questing spirit—can net more discoveries than you can wonder at, right in your own backyard.

F. Eugene Hester; opposite, Tom Myers

175

Photos by Kent & Donna Dannen

Keeping a Record of Your Visitors

Open a naturalist's notebooks and you find them full of sketches—details of a rabbit's nose or a blackberry, scrawls of a thunderhead. To keep your own record of nature's show in the gardens you've grown, you needn't be a Chuck Ripper—one of the artists whose drawings enliven this book, shown here getting an editing from his ground squirrel model. Your simplest doodle can preserve a fragile impression of a creature you may never see quite that way again. It's part of the extra fun of gardening with wildlife.

Appendix

Use the information below in selecting and locating plants, shrubs, and trees in your yard to accommodate both wildlife and landscaping needs. For geographic distribution of these plantings, see page 65.

Name	Height	Flower	Fruit	Value for Wildlife	Site Comments
Flowers and Grasses					
Bristlegrass, *Setaria* spp.	to 5'	July-August, inconspicuous in bristly spike, yellowish-green	July-August, grain	Especially favored by numerous songbirds and gamebirds, ground squirrels; used for browse by mammals.	Damp to dry, open soil; sun.
Filaree, *Erodium cicutarium*	to 15'	July-August, small, purplish-pink	Sept.-Oct., spindle-shaped, splits into pods	Especially favored by goldfinch, pine siskin, ground squirrel, black-tailed deer in western regions.	Dry, well-drained soil, sun.
Panicgrass, *Panicum* spp.	to 6'	July-August, inconspicuous, in feathery cluster	July-September, grain	Especially favored by ground-feeding songbirds and gamebirds.	Dry, well-drained sand and clay.
Sunflower, *Helianthus* spp.	to 12'	July-Sept., large showy head, yellow, brown center	October-November, dry, single-seeded achene	Very nutritious, favored by many songbirds, gamebirds, also by rodents.	Moist, rich soil; sun.
Turkeymullein, *Eremocarpus setigerus*	to 5'	June-July, inconspicuous, in green spike-like cluster	September-October, grain	Favored by songbirds and gamebirds, especially by mourning dove, song sparrow; also used by squirrel.	Does well in all soils.
Tarweed, *Madia elegans*	to 24'	July-August, yellow with brown center	September, dry, single-seeded achene	Favored by chipmunk, ground squirrel; also by Hungarian partridge, American pipit, and other birds of western regions.	Sandy soil.
Bush Clover, *Lespedeza* spp.	to 9'	August, small, purplish-pink	August-October, pod	Especially favored by bobwhite quail, white-tailed deer; used minimally by songbirds.	Open, sandy soil.
Timothy, *Phleum pratense*	to 5'	May-August, inconspicuous, in cylindrical spikes	June-Aug., grain	Favored by many songbirds, gamebirds; also used for cover.	Dry, well-drained soil.
Ragweed, *Ambrosia* spp.	to 9'	July-October, inconspicuous, male and female separate	July-Oct., dark brown or black achene	Especially favored by bobwhite quail, goldfinch, song sparrow, white-throated sparrow, junco, snowbird, redwinged blackbird.	Does well in poor soil.
Knotweed, *Polygonum* spp.	to 5'	May-Nov., inconspicuous or showy, single or grouped	May-Nov., greenish-brown to black achene	Favored by gamebirds, finches, longspurs, sparrows, chipmunks, ground squirrels.	Dry, hard-packed soil; sun-tolerant.
Pokeweed, *Phytolacca americana*	to 12'	July-Oct., white or pinkish cluster	Autumn, dark purple berry	Especially favored by mourning dove, mockingbird, cedar waxwing; also eaten by raccoons.	Dry, well-drained soil; does well in shade.

Name	Height	Flower	Fruit	Value for Wildlife	Site Comments
Low Shrubs and Vines					
Blackberry, *Rubus* spp.	to 6'	April-June, showy, white, clustered	July-August, black clustered drupelets	Especially favored by nearly a hundred species of birds; also by many small mammals for cover and food; also used for winter browse by deer and rabbits.	Moist, well-drained soil.
Oregon Grape, *Mahonia vervosa*	to 3'	Dec.-April, small, yellow terminal cluster	March-June, dark blue berry	Favored by pheasants, eaten by other birds only occasionally; used for browse by hoofed mammals in West.	Sheltered shade.
Pricklypear, *Opuntia* spp.	to 2'	May-June, showy, yellow, pink, or white	Aug.-Oct., large red or purple berry	Fruit, seed, stem favored by 40 or more bird and mammal species in Southwest.	Sandy soil, rocky open places.
Snowberry, *Symphoricarpos albus*	to 5'	May-Sept., pink, clustered	Aug.-Oct., white berry-like drupe	Favored by grouse, pine grosbeak, varied thrush in western regions all winter; used for browse by hoofed mammals, used for cover by mammals and birds.	Dry, rocky soil; shade-tolerant.
Coralberry, *Symphoricarpos orbiculatus*	to 6'	July-August, greenish to purple cluster	September into winter, coral to purple berry cluster	Favored by songbirds and gamebirds, especially pine and evening grosbeak, brown thrasher, robins, towhees, ruffed grouse, pheasants; also used for cover and nesting by sparrows.	Wet or dry, sun or shade; does well in limestone or clay.
Virginia Creeper, *Parthenocissus quinquefolia*	Vine	June-August, small, greenish, clustered	Aug.-Feb., blue berry	Favored by mockingbird, yellow-shafted flicker, sapsuckers, mice, chipmunks, skunks; used for winter browse.	Moist, well-drained soil; sun.
Bayberry, *Myrica pensylvanica*	to 9'	May-June, inconspicuous, clustered	Sept.-Oct., gray, waxy, berry-like nut	Especially favored by tree swallow, myrtle warbler; used by other songbirds and gamebirds for cover and food.	Well-drained, dry, sandy soil; sun or shade.
Dwarf Juniper, *Juniperus* spp.	to 4'	May-June, none; cone-bearing	Sept.-Dec. bluish-black berry-like cone	Favored by numerous birds and mammals, especially cedar waxwing, evening grosbeak; used for cover by robin, sparrows, mockingbird, junco, warblers.	Moderately moist, loamy soil; also dry rocky places.
Western Juniper, *Juniperus occidentalis*	to 6'	Same as above	Sept.-Oct., black, oval, berry-like cone	Same as above.	Same as above.
Common Spicebush, *Lindera benzoin*	to 12'	April-May, small, yellow, clustered spike, male and female separate	July-Sept., red drupe	Especially favored by thrushes, used minimally by other birds.	Well-drained, moist soil.
Gooseberry, *Ribes* spp.	to 5'	April-August, small, green to purple	June-Sept., reddish-purple to black berry	Favored by robin, cedar waxwing, American magpie, catbird, many gamebirds; used for browse by white-tailed deer and moose in western regions.	Moist soil, open places; often along a stream.

Name	Height	Flower	Fruit	Value for Wildlife	Site Comments
Mapleleaf Viburnum *Viburnum acerifolium*	to 7'	May-August, small, clustered	July-Oct., red to black or purple drupe	Favored by grouse; browse for deer and rabbits.	Moist soil; shade.
Greenbrier, *Smilax* spp.	Vine	April-June, greenish, clustered	Sept.-Nov., blue-black to red berry	Favored by thrushes, mockingbird, catbird, ruffed grouse; used by black bear, raccoon; for browse by deer.	Moist lowlands.
Bittersweet, *Celastrus scandens*	Vine	May-June, small, green, clustered	Sept.-Dec., orange berry-like capsule, each seed enclosed in pulpy scarlet aril	Favored by gamebirds, minimally by songbirds; ruffed grouse, pheasants, bobwhite quail, bluebird, robin, red-eyed vireo, hermit thrush.	Not particularly shade tolerant.
Alderleaf Buckthorn, *Rhamnus alnifolia*	to 3'	May-June, greenish-yellow	Aug.-Sept., black drupe	Especially favored by pileated woodpecker, catbird, mockingbird, thrushes, especially in Pacific Northwest.	Moist soil, especially swamps and boggy areas.
Sagebrush, *Artemisia* sp.	to 10'	July-October, whitish-gray thick cluster	July-Oct., very small nutlet	Especially favored by sage grouse for food and cover; also used for cover by many small mammals; also eaten by hoofed browsers.	Tolerates moderately alkaline soil; sun; does well in semi-arid areas.
Japanese Honeysuckle, *Lonicera japonica*	Vine	June-October, white to yellow	September-November, black berry	Favored by songbirds and gamebirds for food and cover, especially purple finch, pine grosbeak; also eaten by rabbits and hoofed browsers in winter.	Well-drained soil; shade tolerant.
Large Shrubs					
Winterberry, *Ilex verticillata*	to 20'	June-July, inconspicuous	Sept.-Oct. into winter, red berry-like drupe	Especially favored by mockingbird, thrushes, bluebird, robin.	Acid soil; not very hardy in cold.
Common or Highbush Blueberry, *Vaccinium corymbosum*	to 12'	May-June, small, greenish-white	June-Sept., blue-black berry	Favored by mourning dove, grouse, bluebird, orchard oriole, scarlet tanager, chipmunks, mice.	Acid soil; sun.
Red Osier, *Cornus stolonifera*	to 10'	May-August, white cluster	July-Oct., white drupe	Favored by songbirds and gamebirds; used for browse by large and small mammals.	Well-drained, dry, slightly acid soil; some sun.
Silky Dogwood, *Cornus amomum*	to 10'	June-July, white cluster	Aug.-Oct., bluish drupe	Same as above.	Same as above.
Common Elderberry, *Sambucus canadensis*	to 13'	May-July, flat white cluster	June-Sept., purplish-black berry-like drupe	Favored by 40 species of birds; used by large and small mammals for food and cover.	Well-drained, dry soil; sun or shade.
Manzanita, *Arctostaphylos* spp.	to 20'	Spring, small to showy, white to pink	Fall, reddish-brown drupe	Especially favored by sparrows, evening grosbeak, hooded skunk; used for cover and food by many other birds and mammals in the Southwest.	Well-drained, dry soil; sheltered site; does well in rocky regions.

Name	Height	Flower	Fruit	Value for Wildlife	Site Comments
Fragrant Sumac, *Rhus aromatica*	to 7'	April-July, small, greenish cluster	July-Oct., through winter, dry, red drupe	Favored throughout winter by songbirds and gamebirds; also used by rabbits and white-tailed deer for browse.	Well-drained, dry, acid soil; sun or shade.
Autumn Olive, *Elaeagnus umbellata*	to 12'	May-June, yellowish-white	October into the winter, red drupe	Especially favored by cedar waxwing, robin, evening grosbeak; also used by many other songbirds.	Well-drained, dry soil; sun.
Russian olive, *Elaeagnus angustifolia*	to 12'	May-June, small, yellowish-white	September-October, red drupe	Especially favored by cedar waxwing, robin, evening grosbeak; also used for food and cover by many other birds and small mammals.	Dry, well-drained soil; sun, some shade.
Highbush Cranberry, *Viburnum trilobum*	to 17'	May-July, white, clustered	October into the winter, red berry	Especially favored by game-birds; winter staple for ruffed grouse; good for nesting and roosting.	Rich, well-drained to wet soil.
Tartarian Honeysuckle, *Lonicera tatarica*	to 10'	May-June, showy, pink, white (rarely)	June-Aug., red or yellow (rarely), berry	Especially favored by brown thrasher, catbird, robin, cedar waxwing, purple finch, white-throated sparrow.	Moist or dry soil; full sun.
Firethorn, *Pyracantha coccinea*	to 10'	May-June, small, white, clustered	August into the winter, small, bright orange berry-like pome	Especially favored by catbird, mockingbird, purple finch.	Well-drained, moist soil; sun.
Southern Arrowwood, *Viburnum dentatum*	to 10'	June-August, small, white, clustered	Aug.-Nov., blue-black drupe	Favored by thrushes, flickers, phoebes, ruffed grouse, bluebird, catbird; also used for cover.	Moist soil; sun or shade.
Multiflora Rose, *Rosa multiflora*	to 6'	May-June, showy, white to pink, clustered	Aug.-Sept., hip	Favored by songbirds and gamebirds in winter, especially by bluebird, robin, cedar waxwing, white-throated sparrow, junco, tree sparrow, catbird, bobwhite, pheasants.	Clearings, roadsides, woods, borders.

Small Trees

Name	Height	Flower	Fruit	Value for Wildlife	Site Comments
Flowering Dogwood, *Cornus florida*	to 40'	March-June, small, yellowish-green clustered between showy white bracts	Aug.-Oct., red drupe	Favored by songbirds and gamebirds; used for browse by large and small mammals.	Well-drained, dry, slightly acid soil; some sun.
Red Cedar *Juniperus virginiana*	to 40'	None; cone-bearing	Fall through spring, whitish-to blackish-green berry-like cone	Favored by numerous birds, including finches, grosbeaks, jays, waxwings; used for nesting and cover by robin, mockingbird, sparrows; also used by winter browsers.	Well-drained, dry soil; sun.
Western Red Cedar, *Juniperus scopulorum*	to 50'	Same as above	Same as above	Same as above.	Rich, moist soil; sun.

Name	Height	Flower	Fruit	Value for Wildlife	Site Comments
Wild Black Cherry, *Prunus serotina*	to 60'	April-June, white	Aug.-Sept., purplish-black drupe	Favored by numerous songbirds and gamebirds, small and large mammals.	Well-drained, dry soil; sun or shade.
Choke Cherry, *Prunus virginiana*	to 30'	Same as above	Same as above	Same as above.	Same as above.
Scarlet-fruited Hawthorn, *Crataegus coccinea*	to 30'	May-June, whitish-pink	Aug.-Oct., small, red pome	Favored by cedar waxwing, fox sparrow; used for nesting by many birds.	Neutral, often poor soil.
Hawthorn, *Crataegus* sp.	Same as above	May-June, white	October, small, greenish to red pome	Same as above.	Same as above.
American Holly, *Ilex opaca*	to 30'	June-July, inconspicuous, yellowish-green, male and female separate.	August-June into winter, red drupe	Especially favored by bluebird, catbird, mockingbird, robin, brown thrasher, thrushes; used for cover by these and other songbirds.	Acid soil; quite hardy, need male and female plant.
Mesquite, *Prosopis juliflora*	to 25'	May-July, small, greenish, yellow spikes	Sept.-Oct., green pod	Especially favored by gambel quail, rabbits, skunks, various rodents in the Southwest.	Well-drained, dry soil; sun.
Persimmon, *Diospyros virginiana*	to 50'	May-June, small, yellowish	Sept.-Oct., large orange-red berry	Especially favored by many species; especially catbird, robin, cedar waxwing, opossum, and other mammals.	Well-drained, dry soil; sun; need male and female plant.
Downy Serviceberry, *Amelanchier arborea*	to 25'	April-June, white, elongated cluster	June-July, reddish-purple berry-like pome	Especially favored by thrushes, crows, chipmunks, squirrels; also used by many songbirds.	Well-drained, moist soil; sun.
Smooth Serviceberry, *Amelanchier laevis*	to 30'	Same as above	May-Aug., same as above	Same as above.	Same as above.
American Crabapple, *Pyrus coronaria*	to 30'	March-May, showy, pink or white	Sept.-Nov., yellowish-green pome	Especially favored by pheasants, purple finch, cedar waxwing, red fox, rabbits.	Well-drained soil; sun.
Red Mulberry, *Morus rubra*	to 60'	May-June, inconspicuous	June-Aug., dark purple berry-like fruit	Favored by many songbirds, especially orioles, mockingbird.	Well-drained, dry soil; sheltered site.
White Mulberry, *Morus alba*	to 60'	Same as above	June-July, white berry-like fruit	Same as above.	Same as above.
Cabbage Palmetto, *Sabal palmetto*	to 80'	May-July, white, clustered	Oct.-Nov., black, oval-shaped drupe	Favored by robins, fish crow, raccoon in the Southeast.	Well-drained, dry soil; sun.

Large Trees

Name	Height	Flower	Fruit	Value for Wildlife	Site Comments
American Mountain-ash, *Sorbus americana*	to 40'	May-June, white, flat-topped cluster	Aug.-Sept., reddish-orange, berry-like pome	Used minimally by some species of birds and mammals, especially gamebirds.	Well-drained, dry soil; sun.

Name	Height	Flower	Fruit	Value for Wildlife	Site Comments
Red Maple, *Acer rubrum*	to 50'	March-April, small, scarlet to yellow cluster	May-July, brown, winged seed (samara)	Especially favored by squirrels, chipmunks, evening grosbeak.	Swampy regions.
Sugar Maple, *Acer saccharum*	to 60'	May-June, small, yellowish cluster	June-Sept., same as above	Same as above.	Well-drained, fertile soil, even in rocky places.
Ashleaf Maple or Boxelder, *Acer negundo*	to 75'	April-May, small, yellowish cluster	Sept.-Oct., same as above	Same as above.	Well-drained soil.
California Black Oak, *Quercus kelloggii*	to 125'	April-June, female is inconspicuous, male is long, slender catkin	September, acorn	Great importance to wildlife; especially favored by gamebirds and songbirds; also used by many mammals and hoofed browsers.	Well-drained soil; sun.
Live Oak, *Quercus virginiana*	to 60'	Same as above	Same as above	Same as above.	Hardiest in Southeast.
Pin Oak, *Quercus palustris*	to 90'	Same as above	Same as above	Same as above.	Well-drained, dry soil; sun or shade.
White Oak, *Quercus alba*	to 100'	Same as above	Same as above	Same as above.	Well-drained, dry soil; sun or shade.
Pecan, *Carya illinoensis*	to 120'	April-May, inconspicuous	Sept.-Oct., brown nut	Favored by squirrels, foxes, woodchucks, chipmunks.	Well-drained, rich bottomlands.
Loblolly Pine, *Pinus taeda*	to 100'	Spring, none; cone-bearing	3-inch cone	Great importance to wildlife; especially favored by red crossbill, nutcracker, white-hooded woodpecker, pine grosbeak, nuthatches, jays; also fur and game mammals, hoofed browsers; also used for nesting and roosting cover.	Dry, light, sandy soil; does well in poor soil.
Lodgepole Pine, *Pinus contorta*	to 30'	Same as above	1/2-inch cone	Same as above.	Sandy soil; high altitude.
Pinyon Pine, *Pinus edulis*	to 25'	Same as above	2-inch cone	Same as above.	Well-drained, dry soil; sun.
Ponderosa Pine, *Pinus ponderosa*	to 150'	Same as above	6-inch cone	Same as above.	Well-drained, dry soil; sun, some shade.
Slash Pine, *Pinus caribaea*	to 100'	Same as above	2-inch cone	Same as above.	Dry, light, sandy soil; does well in poor soils.
White Pine, *Pinus strobus*	to 100'	Same as above	4- to 6-inch cone	Same as above.	Well-drained, moist soil; sun.
Blackgum, *Nyssa sylvatica*	to 100'	April-May, small, greenish	October, blue-black drupe	Favored by over 30 bird species, especially ruffed grouse, prairie chicken, pheasant, wild turkey, robin, pileated woodpecker, mockingbird, brown thrasher, thrushes, flickers, starlings.	Rich, moist bottomlands.
Beech, *Fagus grandifolia*	to 100'	April-May, inconspicuous	Sept.-Oct., triangular nut	Especially favored by squirrels and chipmunks, ruffed grouse, tufted titmouse.	Moist soil; shade, some sun.

Name	Height	Flower	Fruit	Value for Wildlife	Site Comments
American White Birch, *Betula papyrifera*	to 80′	May, female, green, inconspicuous; male is golden, both in catkins	Aug.-Sept., winged nutlet	Especially favored by sharp-tailed grouse, black-capped chickadee, common redpoll, pine siskin; also used by many fur and game mammals, hoofed browsers.	Moist, fertile soil; sun.
Colorado Blue Spruce, *Picea pungens*	to 140′	None; cone-bearing	September, 3- to 4-inch cone	Favored by grouse, crossbills, nuthatches, squirrels, hares; used primarily by northern animals.	Well-drained, light, sandy loam; does well in most soils.
Douglasfir, *Pseudotsuga taxifolia*	to 300′	None; cone-bearing	6-inch cone	Favored by blue grouse, chickadees, squirrels, shrews, white-tailed deer in Northwest.	Well-drained, dry or moist soil; sun or shade.
American Hackberry, *Celtis occidentalis*	to 40′	April-May, small, greenish	Sept.-Oct., dark purple drupe	Favored by many winter birds, especially cedar waxwing, yellow-bellied sapsucker, mockingbird, robin, olive-backed thrush.	Rich, moist soil.
Eastern Hemlock, *Tsuga canadensis*	to 70′	July, none; cone-bearing	October, 1/2 to 3/4-inch cone	Favored by pine siskin, crossbills, chickadees, grouse, squirrels; used for winter cover by ruffed grouse, wild turkey, deer; used for nesting by veery, various warblers, junco.	Well-drained, moist soil; sun or shade.

Backyard Wildlife Program

of the
National Wildlife Federation

Throughout GARDENING WITH WILDLIFE there have been references to the National Wildlife Federation's Backyard Wildlife Program. It is, essentially, an action program which encourages homeowners to create or maintain a miniature refuge on their property and which gives public recognition to those who do. To give readers even more precise information about the program and how they may participate in it, the editors take pleasure in setting forth the following summary of its objectives and procedures.

How does the program operate?

The homeowner submits an application form which outlines the provisions made for wildlife in his yard. If judged by the National Wildlife Federation to be providing food, water, cover, and nesting areas for wildlife on a regular basis, the owner is given a certificate declaring his property to be a National Wildlife Backyard Habitat with a personal registration number.

How does certification help wildlife?

With the owner's permission, the National Wildlife Federation sends a press release to the local newspaper announcing the Federation's official recognition of his or her efforts on behalf of wildlife. The resulting publicity calls attention to the homeowner's environmental contribution and motivates others to do the same. The backyard data being accumulated in the National Wildlife Federation's records of this program is an increasingly valuable source of current wildlife information of a kind which has not been compiled before.

Who may participate?

Any homeowner or member of his or her family who is 13 years of age or older.

What size lot is required?

The property enrolled may not exceed three acres in size, but may be as small as a townhouse garden.

How does a homeowner participate?

He secures from the National Wildlife Federation an application form on which he is asked to give the following information:

How food is provided for wildlife

- the number of berry-, nut-, or seed-producing trees, shrubs, and herbaceous growth, by species, which provide part or all of a year-round food supply.
- the number and type of bird feeders and squirrel feeders in use, whether made or purchased, and the foods with which they are stocked.

How water is provided for wildlife

- by building a water garden, a small pool or a pond; installing a birdbath; or other method —and how the supply of water is maintained; also how the problem of freezing in winter is handled.

How cover is provided

- the species of trees and shrubs growing in hedges or clumps and the species of tall grasses planted; whether brushpiles have been made for birds and mammals, and whether homes for amphibians are provided in rockpiles, stone walls, or brickwork; number and kind of birdhouses which have been bought or built.

How reproductive areas are provided

- provisions made for nesting places for birds, including nest boxes; also squirrel den trees and boxes; and the provision of a pool for the breeding of amphibians and fish.

Other methods of attracting wildlife

- examples: creating dust baths for birds or putting out artificial nest-building materials.

What proof of the effectiveness of the backyard refuge is required?

Applicant is asked to list birds, mammals, amphibians, reptiles, insects, and fish observed; and to submit photographs or rough scale drawing of the yard, its plantings and other wildlife provisions.

Is present owner of property required to do the planting and make all other habitat improvements himself?

Not at all. His responsibility is to create a habitat or to maintain the habitat which former owners may have established, improving it wherever possible.

How are the costs of the program borne?

A project enrollment fee of $2.00 is paid by each applicant to help defray costs of program literature, staff time devoted to review and evaluation of applications, record keeping, and postage.

How is application form secured?

For a free copy, write to: Backyard Wildlife Program
National Wildlife Federation
1412 16th St., N.W.
Washington, D.C. 20036

For Further Reading

...about birds and mammals

Arbib, Robert and Tony Soper, *The Hungry Bird Book*, Taplinger Publishing, New York, 1971.

Barkalow, Frederick S., Jr. and Monica Shorten, *The World of the Gray Squirrel*, J. B. Lippincott Company, Philadelphia, 1973.

Davison, Verne E., *Attracting Birds from the Prairies to the Atlantic*, Thomas Y. Crowell Company, 1967.

McElroy, Thomas P., Jr., *The New Handbook of Attracting Birds*, Alfred A. Knopf, New York, 1960.

Morgan, Ann Haven, *Field Guide to Animals in Winter*, G. P. Putnam's Sons, New York, 1939.

Reilly, Edgar, *The Audubon Illustrated Handbook of American Birds*, McGraw-Hill, New York, 1968.

Walker, Z. V., *The Mammals of North America*, The Johns Hopkins Press, Baltimore, 1964.

Wetmore, Alexander, *Song and Garden Birds of North America*, National Geographic Society, Washington, D.C., 1964.

...about insects and spiders

Headstrom, Richard, *Spiders of the United States*, A. S. Barnes and Company, New York, 1973.

Lanham, Url, *The Insects*, Columbia University Press, New York, 1964.

Linsenmaier, Walter, *Insects of the World*, McGraw-Hill, New York, 1972.

...about plant life and gardening

Fenten, D. X., *Greenhorn's Guide to Gardening*, Grosset and Dunlap Publishers, New York, 1969.

Flemer, William, *Nature's Guide to Successful Gardening and Landscaping*, Thomas Y. Crowell Company, New York, 1972.

Grimm, William C., *Recognizing Native Shrubs*, Stackpole Books, Harrisburg, 1966.

Hunter, Beatrice Trum, *Gardening Without Poisons*, Houghton Mifflin Company, Boston, 1964.

Murphy, Richard C. and William E. Meyer, *The Care and Feeding of Trees*, Crown Publishers, New York, 1969.

Taylor, Norman, ed., *Taylor's Encyclopedia of Gardening*, Houghton Mifflin Company, Boston, 1961.

Wyman, Donald, *Shrubs and Vines for American Gardens*, MacMillan Company, London, Revised and Enlarged Edition, 1969.

...about pond life

Amos, William H., *The Life of the Pond*, McGraw-Hill, New York, 1967.

Andrews, William A., ed., *Guide to the Study of Freshwater Ecology*, Prentice-Hall, Englewood Cliffs, 1972.

Hotchkiss, Neil, *Common Marsh, Underwater and Floating-leaved Plants of the United States and Canada*, Dover Publications, 1972.

...about wildlife habitat

Billard, Ruth Sawyer, *Birdscaping Your Yard*, Department of Environmental Protection, State of Connecticut, Hartford, 1972.

Martin, Alexander, Herbert S. Zim and Arnold L. Nelson, *American Wildlife and Plants—A Guide to Wildlife Food Habits*, McGraw-Hill, New York, 1951.

McElroy, Thomas P., Jr., *The Habitat Guide to Birding*, Alfred A. Knopf, New York, 1974.

Vosburgh, John, *Living With Your Land*, Charles Scribner's Sons, New York, 1968.

Index

Text references appear in lightface type, illustrations in **boldface**

A

Acorns: 66,98
Ambush bugs: **27**
Amphibians: 23, 24, 54-55, 117; attracting, 99, 156; water for, 101
Ant lions: 28
Anting: 29
Ants: 27, 29, **36, 37,** 159; observing, 25
Aphids: 17, 27, 29, 42
Apple trees: 156
Apples: 13, 129
Arrowwood: 129
Asters: 125
Autumn olive bushes: 53, 57, 61, 62, 133

B

Backyard Wildlife Habitat Program: 18, 71-72; participation in, 184-185
Backyard wildlife habitats: 19, 49, 55; enjoying, 26; log book for, 23, 176; maintaining, 70, 121-136; planning, 22, 51-53, 56-65, 69
Barberry bushes: 130
Bass: 50
Bats: 122, 166; problems with, 158, 159
Bayberry bushes: 56, 58, 64, 130
Bears: 18, **19**
Beech trees: 56
Beechnut trees: 98
Bees: 17, 28, **40,** 41, **45,** 113; identifying, 27
Beetles: 26, 27, **58,** 159
Begonias: 67, 131
Berries: 26, 85, 126, 130, 133, 144
Birch trees: 56, 156
Bird feeders: **8, 10, 12,** 50, 53, 67, 73, **91, 92, 93, 94, 95,** 98, 125, 130, 131, **162;** building, 89, 93-95, 162; placing, 95; posts for, 96, 97; protecting, 95, **163.** *See also:* Hummingbirds: feeders; Suet feeders

Birdbaths: **9, 13, 14, 31, 53, 59,** 89, 101, **113,** 125, 135; cleaning, 123; heating, 130
Birdhouses: **6, 8, 15, 16,** 63, **122,** 126, 130, 157, 163; building, 89, **96, 97,** 135; cleaning, 122, 131; dimensions (chart), 97; placing, 96; posts for, **96,** 97
Birds: 21, 22, 23, 24, 26, 54-55, 70; attracting, 60, 61, 67-69, 101, 122, 125, 133, 156, 167; chicks, 126; controlling, 158, 160, 161; eggs, 155; feeding, 8, 60, 62, 66, 73, 90, 91, 93, 94, 95, 126-133, 177-183; feeding (chart), 92; behavior, 30; identifying, 17, 29-31; injured, 126; list of, 97; migration of, 29, 60, 63, 72, 82, 83, 123, 125, 126, 129, 130, 131; nests and nesting, 8, 80, 81, 125, 126, 128, 135, 158, 164; observing, 25, 29, 30, 32, 61, 62, 132, 133, 173; photographing, 94, 135, *See also:* Wildlife: problems with, 158, 164; songs of, 29, 30; water for, 101, 104, 105, 125
Bitterns: 29
Bittersweet bushes: 133
Black locust seeds: 66
Blackberries: 126, 162
Blackbirds: 29, 123
Bluebirds: 80, **81,** 123, 130
Bluegill sunfish: **50**
Blue jays: 32, **84,** 85, **86-87,** 94, 132, **162**
Bobolinks: **28,** 29, 129
Brambles: 156
Brazilian pepper trees: 64
Bristlegrass: 133
Brushpiles: **13,** 98, 99, 131-132, **134,** 135, 143, 156
Butterflies: 23, 28, **44-47,** 54-55, 123, 135, 156; catching, 175; observing, 128

C

Camellias: 162
Cardinal flowers: 67
Cardinals: **12,** 17, 21, 29, 55, 60, **130,** 132; feeding, 91
Catbirds: 29, 55, 126, 128; identifying, 31
Caterpillars: **22, 29,** 49, 127
Cedar berries: 26
Cedar waxwings: **26, 84,** 85, 126, 128

D

Centipedes: 23; identifying, 24
Chameleons: 127
Chapparal: 64
Cherries: 66, 98, 156, 162
Cherry trees: 133
Chestnut trees: 19
Chickadees: 32, 55, 83, 85, 90, 127, 132; feeding, 91, 94; identifying, 31
Chimneys: 161; cleaning, 159; problems with, 158-159, 161; screening, **159**
Chipmunks: **2, 11,** 24, 26, 55, 59, 64, 123, **136, 140, 141;** attracting, 98, 99; feeding, 66, 98; hibernation of, 140; observing, 126; rockpiles for, 98, **99**
Chokeberries: 128
Christmas trees: 133
Chrysanthemums: **10,** 127
Cicadas: 22, 27, 28, 129
Click beetles: 28, 29, **58,** 127
Clover: 66
Columbine: 67, 125
Compost piles: **129**
Conifers: 55, 66, 121
Cosmos: 125
Cowbirds: 31, **81,** 123
Coyotes: 64
Crabapple trees: 58, 162
Cranberry bushes: 130, 133
Craneflies: catching, 175
Crayfish: 24, 104, 115, 155
Creepers: 69
Crested flycatchers: 126
Crickets: 27, 28
Crocus: 125, 130
Crossbills: 55
Crustaceans: 23, 24
Currants: 162
Cypress trees: 59

Daffodils: 125, 130
Dahlias: 131
Damselflies: 28
Deer: **14, 66, 144-145;** feeding, 13, 66; footprint of, **172**
Dogwood trees: 56, 57, 98, 128, 133, 162
Doodlebugs: **27**
Dragonflies: 28, 55, 101, **112,** 113, 128; nymph, 28, 113, 128
Ducks: 29, 69, 72, **73, 118-119, 128-129**

E

Edge effect: 69
Efts: *See:* Newt, red-spotted
Elaeagnus bushes: 162
Elderberries: 61, 129, 162
Elm trees: 19
Evening primrose: 67

F

Fairy shrimp: 24, **108,** 111
Feeding stations: 55, 67, 135; *See also:* Bird feeders; Hummingbirds: feeders; Squirrel feeders
Fences: 17, 128, 156-157, 162, 167
Fertilizers: 122, 123, 129
Finches: 17, 29, 32, 55, 60, 133; *See also:* Goldfinches
Fireflies: 28, 127; catching, 175
Firethorn bushes: 30, 133; *See also:* Pyracantha
Fish: 101, 103, 104, 123, 128; *See also:* Goldfish
Fisher spiders: **110,** 111
Fleas: 125
Flickers: 60, 125, **157**
Flies: **27,** 28, 113, 125, 159; catching, 175
Flower gardens: 18, 68; fertilizing, 124; maintaining, 124, 131; protecting, 128
Flower spiders: **27**
Flowers: 19, 21, 51, 53, 59, 70, 125; chart of, 177; planting, 122, 125, 130; protecting, 131; selecting, 51, 63, 65, 133; transplanting, 130
Flycatchers: 29
Four-o-clocks: 125
Foxes: 29, 124, 166
Frogs: **11,** 55, 69, 101, **104, 107, 111,** 115, **117,** 155; catching, 175; *See also:* Tadpoles; Toads
Fruit trees: 133, 160; fertilizing, 124; protecting, **161;** spraying, 122, 135

G

Gardening books: 136
Gardens: 7, 23; *See also:* Flower gardens; Vegetable gardens
Geese: **82,** 128, 130
Gladiolus: 67, 131
Goldfinches: 60, 126, 128; *See also:* Finches
Goldfish: 103, 104, **106,** 130; *See also:* Fish
Grackles: 29, 90; identifying, 31
Grapes: 162
Grasses: 19, 21, 122, 126, 156; chart of, 177; importance of, 29, 99, 167; native, for lawns, 70; nesting material, 27; selecting, 63, 65
Grasshoppers: 27
Greenbrier: 66
Grosbeaks: **16,** 17, 29, 32, **94,** 135
Groundhogs: **70**

H

Hackberries: 66, 130, 162
Hardwood trees: 19, 55, 64
Hawks: 69, 72, 123, 124, 162
Hawthorn bushes: 133
Hazelnuts: 66
Hedges: 29, 70; importance of, 61-62, 167; *See also:* Shrubs
Heeling plants: **123**
Hemlock: 66
Herons: 69, **115**
Hibiscus: 67, 68
Hickory nuts: 66
Holly: 57, 59, 61, 132, 133, 162
Honeysuckle: 67, 126, 133
Hummingbirds: 31, **67, 76-77, 78, 79,** 126, **128;** attracting, 67; feeders, 67, 78, 126; nests, **76-77; 78, 79;** observing, 128
Hyacinths: 125, 130

I

Indigo buntings: 126, 130
Inkberries: 130
Insecticides: 127
Insects: 23, 26-27, **27,** 45, **104;** camouflage of, **29;** eaten by other wildlife, 54-55, 67, 69, 98, 113, 127, 129, 175; identifying, 24, 25, 28; controlling, 125, 127; observing, 28
Iris: 8, **9**
Ivy: 161

J

Jewelweed: 67
Juncos: 29, 126, 132; identifying, 31

K

Katydids: **10,** 28, **29,** 129
Killdeer: 123
Kingbirds: 130

L

Lacewings: 29
Ladybugs: 17, 29, **42-43,** 127
Larkspur: 125
Laurel: 56
Lawns: 29, 59, 68, 70; fertilizing, 122, 124; reseeding, 124
Lespedeza: 66
Lettuce: 13, 127
Lilacs: 51, 62, 67
Lilies: 124, 130
Live trapping: **51,** 154, 155, **158-159,** 160
Lizards: 98
Lombardy poplars: 64
Lotus: 101

M

Magnifying glass: 25, 29, **170**
Mammals: 23, 54-55, 62, 70, 135, 167; identifying, 24; observing, 25; water for, 101, 104
Manatees: 21
Manzanita: 67
Maple trees: 127, 156
Marigolds: **125**
Mayflies: 28
Meadowlarks: 125
Mice: 18, 24, **122;** 129, 147; *See also:* Rats
Millipedes: 23; identifying, 24
Mimosa trees: 126, 132
Minnows: **110,** 111, 113
Mockingbirds: 21, 29, 49, 51, 62, 132, 161; attracting, 162; identifying, 31

Library of Congress CIP Data
Main entry under title:

Gardening with wildlife.

   Bibliography: p.
   Includes index.
   1. Wildlife attracting. 2. Gardening.
I. National Wildlife Federation.
QL59.G37   639'.92   74-82797
ISBN 0-912186-15-1

National Wildlife Federation

Washington, D.C. 20036

Dedicated to improving the quality of our environment

Thomas L. Kimball, *Executive Vice President*
J. A. Brownridge, *Administrative Vice President*
James D. Davis, *Director, Book Development*

Staff for This Book

Russell Bourne, *Editor*
Alma Deane MacConomy, *Associate Editor*
Jennifer Connor, Sarah Dickson Cutter, *Researcher-Writers*
Mel Baughman, *Production and Printing*

Acknowledgments

The interest and professional competence of many friends brought order, depth, and precision to the enthusiasm with which the editors tackled this book. On behalf of the National Wildlife Federation, the editors gratefully acknowledge the assistance of entomologists, ornithologists, botanists, mammalogists, ichthyologists, herpetologists, zoologists, and biologists at the Smithsonian Institution, the U.S. Department of Agriculture, the U.S. Department of the Interior, the University of Arizona, Skidmore College, the University of California at Berkeley, and at Hunting Creek Fisheries, Inc. in Thurmont, Maryland. Together they provided voluminous data on the identification and life cycles of species of plants and animals. Professional contributions of another sort are listed below.

Lloyd W. Swift, *Special Consultant on Ecology*   Charles O. Hyman, *Designer*
Ned Smith, Chuck Ripper, Elisabeth Ripper, and George Founds, *Illustrators*

For translating the idea of gardening with wildlife into concepts and procedures anyone could adapt to his own backyard, the editors wish to thank their distinguished authors:

Roger Tory Peterson, art director of the *National Wildlife Federation*
George Reiger, associate editor of *National Wildlife* and *International Wildlife* magazines
Len Buckwalter, author of articles and books on home improvement
George H. Harrison, managing editor of *National Wildlife* and *International Wildlife* magazines
Donald O. Cunnion, free-lance writer and former garden editor of *Country Gentleman* and *Town-Journal* magazines
Jack Ward Thomas, wildlife biologist, lecturer, and writer
Richard M. DeGraaf, wildlife biologist, lecturer, and writer
David F. Robinson, free-lance author who wrote the portfolio essays

The editors also wish to thank the editors of *National Wildlife, International Wildlife,* and *Ranger Rick's Nature Magazine* for their cooperation.

Finally, the editors wish to acknowledge the contribution of gardeners across the land whose letters, encouragement, and questions made us know this book was needed by both experienced and inexperienced gardeners who care about wildlife.